Edward Davies

An Illustrated Handbook on Africa

Giving an Account of it's People, Climate, etc.

Edward Davies

An Illustrated Handbook on Africa

Giving an Account of it's People, Climate, etc.

ISBN/EAN: 9783744752862

Printed in Europe, USA, Canada, Australia, Japan

Cover: Foto ©Andreas Hilbeck / pixelio.de

More available books at **www.hansebooks.com**

AN

ILLUSTRATED

HANDBOOK ON AFRICA.

GIVING AN ACCOUNT OF ITS PEOPLE, ITS CLIMATE, ITS
RESOURCES, ITS DISCOVERIES, AND SOME OF
ITS MISSIONS.

BY

REV. EDWARD DAVIES,

AUTHOR OF "THE CONTRAST BETWEEN INFIDELITY AND CHRISTIANITY,"
"THE GIFT OF THE HOLY GHOST," "LIFE OF FRANCES RIDLEY
HAVERGAL," "LIFE OF REV. THOMAS HARRISON,"
"LIFE OF REV. WILLIAM TAYLOR," "THE
BISHOP OF AFRICA," ETC.

HOLINESS BOOK CONCERN,

READING, MASS.

COPYRIGHT, 1886, BY E. DAVIES.

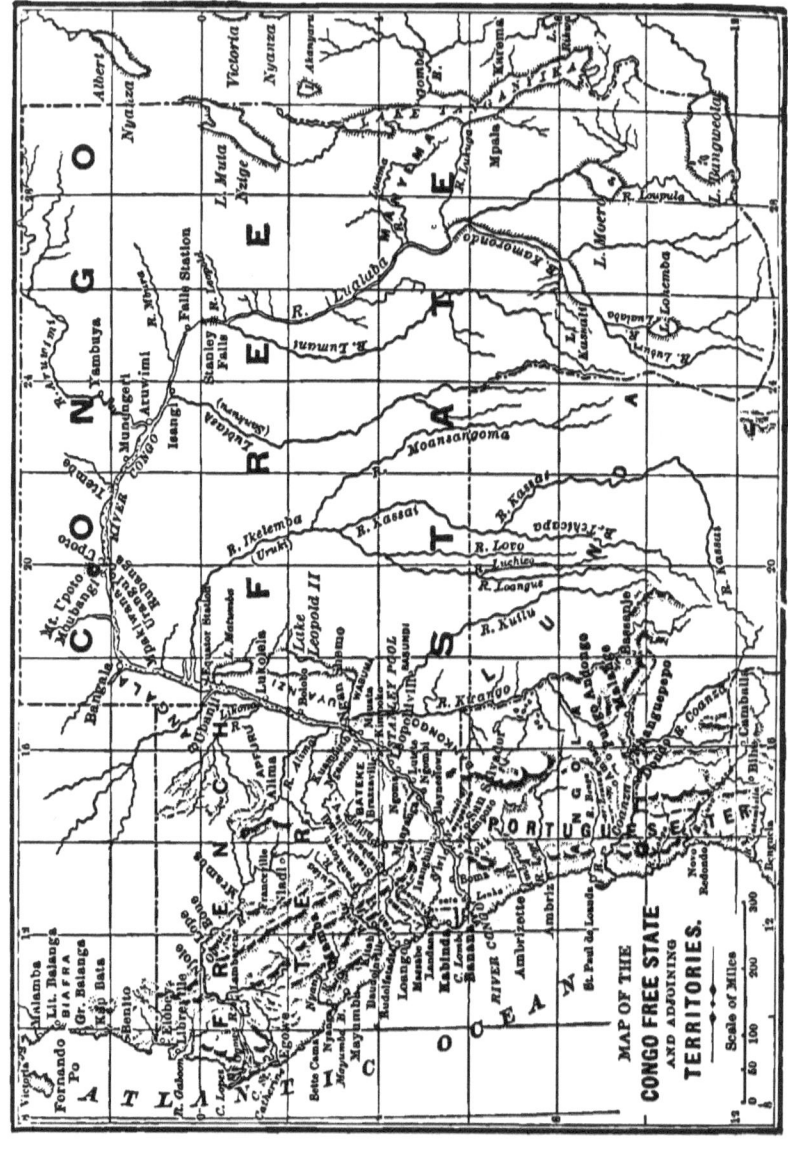

PREFACE.

While in New York, attending the farewell meeting of the third expedition of missionaries for Bishop Wm. Taylor's missions in Africa, we felt a great lack of a HAND BOOK ON AFRICA, which should give the missionaries and their friends a general account of that vast continent, and should especially teach the missionaries *how to live in a tropical climate*, and thus save their precious lives; showing also the prospect of *self-support*, and giving an account of Bishop Taylor's missions, with some of the latest letters, and also the want of a map of Africa that would show, at a glance, the location of those missions, and their relation to one another.

I am greatly indebted to "*The Gospel in all Lands*," to an article in the *Methodist Review*, by Dr. Curry, the editor, on THE NEW CONGO STATE, by Henry M. Stanley, and to Mr. Stanley himself, for his plain and wholesome instructions upon how a European may live on the Congo river, etc.

I have have not written for fame, but that I might be of service, both in the present and in the future, in furnishing a cheap and useful book for the masses, and thereby increase the interest of both missionaries, travellers, and traders in the exploration and salvation of Africa. Many traders, explorers, and missionaries in the tropics have no doubt died before their time for want of just that information that this book contains.

The map in this book has been made from the latest surveys, and is therefore later, and no doubt more correct, than the maps in Mr. Stanley's books.

MAMBA is the first station coming down the coast; it is seventeen miles from MAYUMBA. Brother Benoit is stationed there. He is a successful worker.

KABINDA is the next station, where Brother Judson and his helpers are doing a grand work. ST. PAUL LOANDA is the next station, where an iron house, with a veranda on all sides is soon to be erected for a mission station. Brother Ratcliffe, and L. Fannie

Cummings, and others are stationed there. DONDO is the next station, and is 240 miles from Loanda, at the head of navigation on the Coanza river. (See map.) Brother Davenport and wife are stationed there, and have made the mission self-supporting already.

NHANGUEPEPO is 51 miles further inland, and near the Coanza river. This is the receiving station for missionaries, where Brothers Withey, Gordon, Dolson, and William Mead, and others have an industrial farm and are carrying on quite a business for God and man. They have 2500 acres of land, given to them for mission purposes.

PUNGO ANDONGO is the next station, and is about 37 miles from Nhanguepepo. Some of the wonders of nature surround this station. Brother Wilkes and wife and daughter are the missionaries. They are doing a great work.

MALANGE is about 60 miles from Pungo Andongo, and about 400 miles from Loanda. Dr. Summers, and Brother Samuel Mead and family are doing a good work here, and are looking toward the interior.

Bishop Taylor is planting stations on the Congo river. His first station, according to his last letter, is at Kimpoko, on the north-east corner of Stanley Pool. He expects to plant another station at the junction of the Sankura and Kassai rivers, about 400 miles from Stanley Pool. These he calls the strategetic points for work on the Congo, Kassai, and Sankura rivers.

EDWARD DAVIES.
Reading, Mass., Oct. 30, 1886.

The former editions of this book have met with so much public and private favor, that I have been encouraged to enlarge the fifth chapter, and add a most deeply interesting chapter on Liberia.

THE AUTHOR.
Reading, July 20, 1887.

HAND BOOK ON AFRICA.

CHAPTER I.

AFRICA is one of the five divisions of the globe. Only a small extent of sea separates Africa from Europe. Its coasts lie in sight of the most civilized countries. The valley of the Nile was, in the earliest ages of history, the cradle of commerce, the arts and sciences. But even in the period of Egypt's greatest prosperity, deep night seems to have enveloped the surrounding countries, which were called Negroland. Africa is a vast peninsula, forming a triangle, with its vertex toward the south, containing 12,256,000 square miles. Bounded on the north by the Mediterranean Sea, on the east by Asia, the Red Sea and the Indian Ocean, on the south and west by the Southern and the Atlantic Oceans. It possesses immense chains of mountains, as the Atlas Mountains, the Mountains of the Moon, of Kong and Gupata. Those of the Cape are 5000 feet high. Its great rivers are the Congo, the Nile, the Zambeze, the Niger, and others. It contains a number of large lakes, as the Albert Nyanza, Victoria Nyanza, Lake Tanganika, Lake Leopold II., Lake Nyassa and others.

To the naturalist this country is the first favorite of nature, as far as it respects the riches of the organic world, and the number of giant forms of animals and plants. It can enumerate five times as many quadrupeds as Asia, and three times as many as all America. It excels Asia in the size of its colossal river-horse, (hippopotamus) gigantic giraffe, and large antelopes and apes. That giant of birds, the ostrich, is exclusively indigenous to Africa. But the camel is the most beneficent gift of nature to Africa, the constitution of which is in every respect adapted to the country and climate. The elephant and rhinoceros, the lion, panther, leopard, ounce, jackal, hyena, wolf, fox, dog, cat, monkey, bat, rat, hare, rabbit, jirboa, bear, horse, ass, zebra, and sheep, some with hair and large fat tails, goats, innumerable varieties of the gazelle, the buffalo, and fallow deer.

The variety of birds are equally innumerable; among which is the crown bird, the most beautiful of the feathered tribe; the flamingo, king fisher, and many kinds of parrots; the peacock, partridge, pheasant, widow and cardinal bird; the cuckoo, the cuculus indicator, turtle doves, pigeons, ducks, geese, etc. The class of reptiles comprises the crocodile and boa-constrictor, with many other serpents. Some innoxious, some highly poisonous. The bays and rivers abound in fish, but the variety is not so numerous as in the northern seas. The shrubs and earth swarm with termites, ants, scolopendras, spiders and caterpillars, while at times passing armies of locusts will obscure the light of the sun. The most beautiful insects abound. Still more extroadinary is the force of vegetation. The earth renders back the seed to the cultivator increased a hundred-fold and produces those immense trees, among which is the baobab or monkey bread tree, whose crown and branches sometimes form a circle 130 feet in diameter, holds the first rank. The splendid white trunk of the ceiba grows almost perpendicularly from the root to the branches, 60 feet, and, with its fine round crown, rises to a height of 120 feet.

ANIMALS, INSECTS AND VEGETATION.

In Africa as in America, the torrid zone produces plants and fruits, at the same time the most nutritious and the most refreshing and most wholesome. The antiseptical quality appertains to the fruits of the palm, banana, orange, shaddock, pine-apple, tamarind, and to the juice and leaves of the baobab. The best butter, likewise an excellent medicine, may be procured from the shih or butter tree, in the interior of the west of Africa, and the groundnuts of Whidah ripen in six weeks from the time of sowing. The vegetable productions used for sustenance are principally wheat, barley, millet, rice, yams, lotus berries, gum Senegal, dates, figs, and various kinds of spices, and especially sugar cane; for drink, coffee is used, palm wine from the female palm tree, the milk of cocoanuts, and Cape wine; for clothing, cotton, hemp, and some flax are used. Here thrive the papau, the pomegranate, five kinds of pepper, the best indigo, from which is procured dragon's blood, the tallow tree, the best wood for dyeing and cabinet work, innumerable spices, etc.

Some suppose, yea, declare, that Africa has more gold than any other portion of the earth. Iron is found in most parts of Africa, but not the other metals; saltpetre, fuller's earth, and emery in abundance; amber is found on the coasts. The want of salt, except in a few regions, is severely felt.

The interior of the country must be very populous, since within two centuries and a half it has contributed 40,000,000 of vigorous men to the slave trade, and, notwithstanding, still abounds with people. Even the countries along the coast are thickly populated. Morocco alone is supposed to have 17,000,000 inhabitants. The people of Africa belong to two branches of the human family: to the black, or Ethiopic race, which extends from Joliba to the southern extremity, comprising, notwithstanding their tawny complexions, the Hottentots; and the Caucasian race which includes the natives of Barbary, Copts the Arabs or Moors, the Agaziones or Abyssinians, and the nations of Nubia. The Arabs are not to be regarded as the aborigines of Africa, but they have scattered themselves and become occupants of the greater part of the north and west. The Arabic is the leading language throughout all the the north. The Berber and Shelluh tongues are spoken in the Barbary states and along the Atlas mountains. The Mandingo language is used from the Senegal to the Joliba and most of the eastern coast. On the western coast a corrupt Portuguese is heard; in the region of Abyssinia, the Tigre and Amhara tongues prevail. The languages of the blacks are almost as multifarious as the nations. In Sahara alone, forty-three dialects are said to be spoken.

Mohammedanism has diffused itself over vast territories, but the christian religion is finding its way among the peoples and tribes of Africa.

FETICHISM.

The most disgusting fetichism prevails among most of the Negro nations, demanding for many of its votaries, human sacrifices. The fetich is a material thing, living or dead, which is made the object of brutish and superstitious worship. It may be a stone, a tin, an animal, or a graven image. Indeed there are so many objects of worship (or fear), that it would be quite impossible to enumerate them. Many of the natives wear some of these fetiches on their person, usually fastened with a string, that is tied round the neck. They consist of small pieces of wood, carved into the likeness of some person or animal, real or imaginary — the teeth of a young hippopotamus, the claws of a lion or tiger. Often a piece of clay shaped into some strange form and dried in the sun or burned in fire. They do not worship the fetich with prayer or praise or by any emotion of love. Their religion is one of fear, and they trust in the fetich to deliver them from disease, pestilence, and the power of their enemies. Very often, as we walk along their paths, at the top of a hill we see a fetich in the form of a pile of stones, which has been accumulated by every traveller, as he came up the hill, picking up a stone and then throwing it on the pile. If one tribe should suffer a series of defeats from another tribe, they would think the successful one had a stronger fetich than they, and would do all in their power to find out what it was. If they failed in this, they would endeavor to institute one endowed with superior power.

Several years ago, the king at Bonny, on the West Coast of Africa, had been repeatedly defeated by a neighboring tribe; he resorted to one of his principal villages, and found it in imminent danger of being captured by the enemy; he then summoned all the fetich men (or priests) in his tribe, and informed them of the situation, at the same time telling them that they must find some fetich more powerful than any then in their possession. The people were called together, and after several hours of wild and strange gesticulations, in which they were worked up to a pitch of excitement where they were ready to do anything, the priests commanded that two holes should be dug in front of the crowd and near together, twelve inches square, and about three feet deep.

This being done, they selected a beautiful girl from the company, and directed that she should be brought to the spot, and one of her feet placed in each of these holes. They then ordered a number of men to take moist clay, and build it up around her from the ground, packing it closely against her. This was continued until she was completely buried alive. The multitude then gave a loud shout, and dispersed. Tidings of this new fetich were carried to their enemies, and they were so afraid of it that they ceased to trouble them any more. For years this clay stood there, regarded by all who knew of it as the greatest fetich known.

All of the native tribes believe that the white man has a fetich superior to theirs, and this often preserves the lives of the whites, when they would otherwise be destroyed, as the natives are afraid that the powerful fetich of the white man would visit them with some terrible affliction, if they did anything against his worshipers. According to their belief, no one dies from natural causes, but the deceased has always been bewitched by another member of the tribe, who must be found out by the priest and put to death.

NATIVE RELIGION.

"At a first glance, inexperienced men will say that the native tribes of Central Africa worship nothing, and that consequently they have no relig-

NATIVE RELIGION.

ious belief. A brief residence, however, will convince one that there is a something to which deference is paid, and before which the natives tremble with awe. The Waguha have no temples, no altars, no sacred groves, but at the door of every hut stands a miniature hut. 'Here,' say they, ' dwell the Wazimu, the disembodied spirits of our ancestors, whose favor we seek, whose protection we crave.' Tribes along the Zambezi have a distinct idea of a Supreme being, Maker and Governor of all things, whom they call ' Morimo.' The doctrine of transmigration finds expression in snake, monkey and crocodile worship. Retribution shines forth in the belief of the Waguha, that at death they go into the sunset, there to be judged by a great Being, with whom they will live if approved, from whose presence they will be cast out if condemned. A recent traveller met six men slaves on their way to the coast, singing as if they did not feel the weight and degradation of the slave sticks. 'Why so merry?' said he. They answered: 'We rejoice at the thought of coming back after death and haunting and killing those who have sold us.'

But over all the religious beliefs of the Central African rests a dense cloud of superstition. He trembles before the witch-doctor. He kills his own wife when he imagines her bewitched. He kills one child because it cuts its upper front teeth before the lower. He kills another child when it turns from one side to the other in sleep. The ghost-like medicine man, the universal demi-god of savage nations, with his hidden miscellany of dead lizards, hide, nails of the dead, lion's claws. and vulture-beaks, stalks through the village imparting strange efficacy to claw or bone, stick or stone. And as beneath the dull, leaden skies of the distant north there are believed to be structures haunted by ghosts and goblins, so here the forest, with its tenantry of owls and bats, is the abode of malignant spirits, and the rustling of the foliage at eventide is their mysterious dialogue. Shadowy vagueness and superstitious terror are cardinal elements of Central African religion.

Previous to three hundred years ago, for two centuries Romanism was the ostensible acknowledged religion of Congo. Paganism was interdicted by law, and the severest penalties were inflicted on those known to participate in its rites. At several periods during this time, it would have been difficult, if not impossible to find one adult who had not been baptized. Father Marolla incidently mentions the Jesuits, Dominicans, Franciscans, etc., as contributing to the numerous missionaries at various times sent to the Congo. Among them were some of the most learned and able men that Rome ever sent forth to the Pagan world. When Portugal was at the climax of its power and wealth, the royal sword was ever ready to be unsheathed in the defence of the mission; and the treasures of Portugal were poured out for its support without stint. There were at least one hundred consecrated churches in Congo. But what has become of the church in Congo, with all its resources and power? Ultimately, from a too well-founded dread of being poisoned by the Christians whom they had baptized, the missionaries left the country altogether; and with them the religion they had propagated disappeared simultaneously. The same held good of Loango, and all other stations up and down the coast, except where France and Portugal had retained forts, and manned them."

When Henry M. Stanley was making that wonderful exploration "Through the Dark Continent," he had occasion to fear the very near approach of Mirambo, chief of African banditti, called Ruga Ruga. This chief had spread terror on every side by his sudden and fiery assaults upon anybody and everybody that he thought he could subject to his tyranny.

One day as Stanley and his company were at Urangwa, socially chatting together, the terrible news came that Mirambo was coming, and was only two camps, or twenty miles away, and had an immense army with him. Terror was manifest on every side. Barricades were prepared, sharpshooter's platforms with thick bulwarks of logs were erected. The women hastened to prepare their charms. The Waganda consulted their spirits. Each warrior and elder examined his guns, and loaded them, ramming down the powder with revengeful intentions, while the king hastened backwards and forward with streaming robes.

The king knew that Mr. Stanley had 175 men under his command, with many boxes of ammunition, therefore he said, "You will stop to fight Mirambo, will you not?"

"Not I, my friend; I have no quarrel with Mirambo, and we can not join every nation to fight his neighbors. If Mirambo attacks the village while I am here, and will not go away when I ask him, we will fight. But we can not stop to wait for him."

The king was much distressed, but Stanley and his company went on their way. They travelled to Ungamonizi, whose king was Ndega—a boy of sixteen—and a relative of Mirambo by marriage. This king announced that they had no need to fear Mirambo, for he had just concluded a peace with the Arabs, and was now about to make a friendly visit to his relative.

Now they were all anxious to see this "Mars of Africa, who, since 1871 had made his name feared by both native and foreigner, from Usui to Urari, and from Urinza to Ugogo; a country embracing 9000 square miles."

At dusk the town criers beat on their large drums, and iron bells, and then cried out:

"Listen, O men of Serombo, Mirambo, the brother of Ndega, cometh in the morning. Be ye prepared, therefore, for his young men are hungry. Send your women to dig potatoes, dig potatoes, dig potatoes tomorrow."

At 10 A. M. the next morning the great war drums and the shouts of admiring thousands proclaimed that Mirambo had entered the town. Soon the young men from Mirambo visited the hut of Mr. Stanley. They are the confidential captains of Mirambo's body guard. The chief man of the three said, "Mirambo sends his salaams to the white man. He hopes the white man is friendly to him, and that he does not share the prejudices of the Arabs, and believe Mirambo a bad man. Will he send words of peace to Mirambo?"

"Tell Mirambo," he replied, "that I am eager to see him, and would be glad to shake hands with so great a man. And as I have made strong friendship with Mtesa, Rumanika, and all the kings along the road from Usoga to Unyanwezi, I shall rejoice to make strong friendship with Mirambo also. Tell him I hope he will come and see me as soon as he can."

The next day Mirambo, having sent one of his chiefs to announce his approach, made a visit to Mr. Stanley, who says: "I shook hands with him with fervor, which drew a smile from him, as he said: 'The white man shakes hands like a strong friend.'"

Mr. Stanley says: "His person captivated me, for he was a thorough African gentleman in appearance. Very different from my conception of the terrible bandit who had struck his telling blows at native chiefs and Arabs, with all the rapidity of a Frederick the Great environed by foes."

Mr. Stanley returned his visit in the evening, with about twenty of his principal men. He found him in a bell tent about twenty feet high and twenty-five feet in diameter, with his chiefs around him.

"After quite a friendly conversation, Mauwa Seru was requested to seal their friendship by performing the ceremony of blood-brotherhood between Mirambo and Mr. Stanley. Having caused them to sit facing each other on a straw carpet, he made an incision in each of their right legs, from which he extracted blood, and interchanging it, he exclaimed, 'If either of you break this brotherhood now established between you, may the lion devour him, the serpent poison him, bitterness be in his food, his friends desert him, his gun burst in his hands and wound him, and everything that is bad do wrong to him until he dies.'"

This is blood-brotherhood among the Africans. Thank God there is a blood-brotherhood among the saints of the Most High. We have been redeemed by blood. We are washed in the blood of the Lamb. In heaven we shall sing of the blood, and on earth we enjoy the blessed fellowship of the saints who are of one blood, and of one family,— the family of the household of faith, whose names are written in the Lamb's book of life.

BOSTON UNIVERSITY
COLLEGE OF LIBERAL ARTS
LIBRARY

A VILLAGE ON THE SHORES OF LAKE TANGANIKA.

CHAPTER II.

The eyes of the civilized world are turned toward Africa, yea, the world is waking up to the fact that there is an Africa. The merchant looks that way to see how he can promote commerce and increase his wealth. The missionary turns his eyes thither to see how he can find his way there, and lay deep and strong the foundations of the christian religion, for the benefit of the present and of all coming generations.

Let us not forget that this fair land has already been the arena upon which some of the greatest exploits of history have been enacted. Dr. Curry says, in his reviews of "The *Congo State*," "On the sunny side of Africa the Pharoahs built the Pyramids, and shaped those massive monoliths, the Obelisks and Sphinxes, at which our complacent age gazes with the vacant wonder of children. At the dawn of history, Egypt, the seat of an advanced civilization, was already passing to its decadence. Rome, in her campaign of a thousand years for the conquest and plunder of nations, encountered her most formidable antagonists in Africa, whose warriors carried victory to the very gates of the city of Seven Hills. In mediæval times the Italian republics found their mercantile supremacy challenged by the apparently insignificant States of Barbary, and even when the achievements of the Spanish navigator were sending Spanish hedalgos across the western ocean, intent on spoliation and the spread of the Catholic faith, Portugal was quietly feeling her way down the African coast, till, passing its southern extremity, her adventurous mariners turned again northward, planting their colonies from Mozambique to the Red Sea.

The Africa of which we now purpose to write is, however, quite another than the fringe of small states that lie between the Midland Sea and the wastes of the Sahara and the littorals of the two oceans. We are to consider the vast region hitherto almost entirely unknown, but toward which the eyes of the world are turning — the habitat of that most distinctive of the races of men, the Negro. Even he has been recognized from the earliest times as a social factor, but all along only as a slave. In that relation Egypt has given him a place on her stony monuments; and from that unknown date in the forgotten past till yesterday, the vast unknown regions of Africa were the harvest-field for the supply of the world's slave markets. And now at length the descendants of the slaves stolen from Africa to serve the Anglo-Saxon freemen of America, insular and continental, have strangely become loyal and emancipated subjects of the British sovereign, or else enfranchised freemen of our great Republic. Evidently a beneficent Providence, which contemplated the end from the beginning, was present to overrule the white man's iniquitous lust for gain as manifested in the enslavement of the Negro race; and the denouement of that long-continued tragedy in human history is at length beginning to appear.

The coasts of inter-tropical Africa have for 300 years been possessed and partially occupied by some of the principal nations of Europe; but all the vast interior, beyond a narrow fringe washed by the sea, has remained a *terra incognita*. The school geographies and atlases used by the older half of those now living displayed the whole interior of Africa as an unknown waste, varied only by the mythical "Mountains of the Moon." But with the advent of the current century the deep silence began to be interrupted. Mungo Park pushed his way by Timbuctoo down the Niger, and paid the forfeit of his life for his temerity; and after him the Landers brothers, pursuing the same course, debouched into the ocean, thus solving one of the geographical enigmas of the age. Afterward came Barth, and Baker, and Burton, and Speke, and Grant, and Cameron, and Schweinfurth, and a multitude more, all of whom made tentative efforts toward solving the mysteries of the wonderful unknown land of the black man. A Gallico-American, Du Chaillu, made excursions inward beyond the settlements along the western coast, and rediscovered the gorilla, the cannibals, and the dwarfs. But greater than all these, during the same years the missionary explorer, Livingstone, pierced the continent through and through, and forever broke the spell that had so long made Central Africa an insoluble mystery. After him, inspired by his example, and intent on finding him in his hiding-place, came Stanley, the last, and, measured by results, the greatest, of African explorers. And now the great world has fairly waked up to the fact that there is an African continent, itself a large portion of the solid land of the world, and that it possesses great possibilities in respect to human wants.

It is well, perhaps, that this wonderful land has remained so little known, and therefore unappropriated by any nation, until now, when, under the influence of a better and more christian civilization than has hitherto existed, this newly discovered and still unexplored region of such magnificent proportions may be saved from spoliation, and instead become an arena for the largest development of the industrial, the philanthropic, and the Christian enterprises of the age. And now we see the unprecedented spectacle of a newly discovered country of untold resources preserved and consecrated by the great Christian powers to peace and civilization; and of these things, their processes and the consummation of the scheme for their accomplishment, the two noble volumes now lying before us are the record and the assured prophecy.— This refers to *The New Congo State*, by Henry M. Stanley, in two large volumes.

During the years 1874-77 Mr. Stanley, under the auspices of the proprietor of the "*New York Herald*" and of the "*London Daily Telegraph*," made his famous journey across the "Dark Continent," from Zanzibar to the mouth of the Congo, and reached Europe early in the next year. This man seems to have been himself a scarcely less remarkable discovery than the strange land of which he comes to tell us; but despite his unpromising earlier career, the most cautious and skeptical have been compelled to recognize his personal greatness; and now one of the crowned heads of Europe — Leopold II. of Belgium — becomes the patron of the enterprise of which these books relate the beginnings.

It is not our purpose to retell his story. "Is it not written in the book?" and is not the very

HENRY M. STANLEY.

BOSTON UNIVERSITY
COLLEGE OF LIBERAL ARTS
LIBRARY

air fall of it? It is ours simply, in the proper and least pretentious sense, to review his work, to see and report what has been done, and as we may be able, to set in a clear light some of the salient points of the story, to group together and take account of the more important facts that have been determined, and to make a hasty and necessarily incomplete estimate of the demonstrated possibilities of the things certainly ascertained.

The accomplished results, of which these volumes are the record, make an addition of a new and very important chapter to the world's geographical knowledge. A vast region of inter-tropical Africa, of which heretofore very little was known, and of which only comparatively small parts have been claimed by any foreign power, is now revealed. The remarkable fact is demonstrated that one of the well-known rivers of Western Africa discharges into the Atlantic the drainage of a region equal in area to that of the entire United States east of the Mississippi; that the basin of the Congo extends from the Atlantic Ocean, at about the twelfth degree of east longitude, eastward to the thirtieth degree, three-quarters of the distance across the continent, to the watershed that separates the streams that fall severally into the two oceans. This vast basin lies on both sides of the equator, extending southward more than twelve degrees, over seven hundred geographical miles, and northward through eight degrees, or nearly five hundred geographical miles. The area of this vast basin is thus seen to very considerably exceed a million of square miles, or more than twenty times that of New York or Pennsylvania.

The physical characteristics of this vast area are as remarkable as its extent. From west to east, and equally on both sides of the equator, it appears an unbroken stretch of varied but never mountainous surface, well watered and drained by unfailing rivers, all falling into the Congo, a region of marvellous fertility, producing all the forms of tropical vegetation, and being, of course, the range and haunts of wild animals. There are elephants and buffaloes, lions and tigers, hippopotamuses and crocodiles, giraffes and zebras; while to the hand of industry the earth readily yields the most abundant supplies of whatever is needed for human subsistence.

The vastness of the African continent renders any definite conception of its details exceedingly difficult. The Africa of antiquity and of the Middle Ages was the region now known as North Africa, extending from the Red Sea to the Atlantic Ocean, including the Canary Islands, and from the Mediterranean southward to a little beyond the twentieth degree of north latitude. Of this vast area, the desert of Sahara is the great feature, having Egypt and Nubia and Abyssinia to the eastward, and along the northern littoral, the Barbary States of the recent past and the Africa of Roman history. Beyond the Great Desert is the land of the Berbers and other strange peoples, of whom some account was given in a late number of this Review. South of the Western part of this region is a fairly well defined section, extending from Timbuctoo to the Gulf of Guinea, coming down nearly to the Equator, divided by the Kong Mountains, with the Valley of the Niger on the east, and on the north-west and west the Senegambia country drained by the Senegal, with the Cape Verde Islands off the western coast, and farther southward the British colony of Sierra Leone, the republic of Liberia, and the kingdoms of Ashantee and Dahomey, and the coast towns of the Bight of Benin. This coast is the part of Africa best known in European commercial circles. Eastward from the valley of the Niger, and south of the Desert, is the great central basin, whose water-courses drain an extensive area, and converge in the vast estuary called Lake Tchad. Along the eastern coast from Cape Guardafui to Mozambique is the comparatively narrow belt, two or three hundred miles wide, whose waters flow through inconsiderable streams into the Indian Ocean. Still farther southward (latitude 10 to 20 deg. S.), and extending from the ocean westward, very far toward the Atlantic coast, is the basin of the Zambezi, second in extent only to that of the Congo, having on its south side the well-known states and outlying regions of South Africa, and on the west the Portuguese kingdom of Benguela, whose waters in small rivers fall into the Atlantic. These great natural divisions constitute the entire area of the African continent, except the interior basin, drained by the Congo and its affluents, lying south of the Lake Tchad region and north of the basin of the Zambezi, and extending from the Gulf of Guinea on the west to the "divide" of the water-courses, not far from the Indian Ocean and the head-waters of the Nile.

The Congo River debouches into the Atlantic near the southern extremity of the Gulf of Guinea, about the sixth degree of south latitude, where it was formerly known as the *Zaire*, and recently as the "Livingstone" river, having the state of Loango on the right, and that of Congo on the left, of the river banks. The volume of water that is discharged into the ocean has long been known to be very great, since its current is felt and the discoloration of the water may be seen many leagues from the coast, and the depth of the channel as it enters the sea is a hundred fathoms. Estimates of the volume of the water regularly discharged, made from approximate calculations from the size and velocity of the current, show results agreeing with the requirements of the area drained. The first section of the river — to Boma, seventy miles — is an arm of the sea; and thence upward to Vivi there is a broad, deep, and free channel with a moderate and steady current. Vivi is at the head of the lower river navigation, being at the bottom of the long series of rapids now called the Livingstone Falls, which continue upward nearly two hundred and thirty-five miles through a semi-mountainous region, with more than fifty cataracts of various heights, with long intervening stretches of navigable water to the broad expanse called Stanley Pool. The distance from Banana Point (the port of entry for sea-going vessels) to Boma is about seventy miles; and from Boma to Vivi, at the foot of the rapids, is forty miles more. From Vivi to Leopoldville, the station erected just above the beginning of the cataracts, is about two hundred miles. The vertical descent of the water between Stanley Pool and the river level at Vivi is not far from one thousand feet, and thence to the sea the fall is from two hundred to three hundred feet more.

Stanley Pool is a vast island basin of quiet water, twenty miles in extent from the upper entrance of the great river to its contraction preparatory to its long succession of leaps and tum-

BOSTON UNIVERSITY
COLLEGE OF LIBERAL ARTS
LIBRARY

ON THE WAY TO CENTRAL AFRICA.

bles downward to the Lower Congo. Its breadth is about ten miles; and the whole area is divided into unequal parts by a low wooded island — Buma. From Leopoldville, at the lowest part of Stanley Pool, to the foot of the Stanley Falls, following the river, which is not very crooked, the distance is a thousand and sixty-eight English miles, all without any interruption to navigation, and making a vertical descent of only four inches per mile. Accurate measurements show the elevation of the river at the foot of Stanley Falls to be 1,511 feet above sea level. The navigable extent of the many affluents, from both sides below Stanley Falls, carry the whole mileage up to more than five thousand. In the wide and elevated portion above the Stanley Falls, extending southeastward, is the Lualaba with its great lakes and long affluents, which, however, are navigable only for smaller river crafts, yet largely available for both travel and transportation. On the right of the river, toward the great upland lakes which form the head-waters of the Nile — though the largest and best known of them, the Tanganyika, it is now ascertained sends its waters to the Congo — is a wide expanse of country of which as yet very little is known beyond its great physical characteristics. The outflow of water from Lake Tanganyika, in passing over two hundred miles westward, makes a descent of fully twelve hundred feet, and the south-western shore of that lake rises to an elevation of twenty-five hundred feet above the lake's surface, so making that region the highest land in the Congo basin, a kind of inter-tropical Switzerland. The whole area of the region now called, by anticipation, the State of Congo, is not less than a million and a half square miles, every part of it abundantly watered and remarkably fertile, everywhere traversed by water-ways, and productive beyond computation of whatever is requisite to human subsistence and to the demands of an advanced civilization.

Can Europeans live there?

The climatic conditions of this broad land are no doubt matters of primary interest, and especially since the notion has become prevalent that the climate of inter-tropical Africa has effectually forbidden the incoming of European and American residents. Because it is inter-tropical, and also a level country, the Congo land is, of course, a land of perpetual summer. Observations made at Vivi, for the year 1882, show a maximum upward range of ninety-four degrees (Fahrenheit) in February and May, while June, July and August reached only eighty-six, eighty-four, and eighty-five degrees, respectively. The minimum temperature that year was, in July and August, fifty-six degrees; in June, sixty; in May and September, sixty-seven; in January and December, seventy. Here, as everywhere else, there is among the natives much more dread of the cold than of the heat. The rain-fall for the same year equalled about forty-one and a half inches, of which more than half fell in November, December and January. February, March, April, and May made an aggregate of nineteen inches, while June, July, August, and September, constituting the dry season, were almost absolutely without rain, and yet these months constituted the coolest season of the year. Though cloudy weather usually prevails in all seasons, yet the rains are intermittent and seldom amount to half an inch in twenty-four hours. Moderate winds prevail at nearly all seasons of the year.

Questions that may be asked respecting the salubrity of the climate cannot be answered in a single word. The fact that there is found through all this region a somewhat numerous population (estimated at not less than fifty millions) of stalwart and muscular people, that there are old men of eighty or over, still sufficiently active to be recognized as kings or heads of their tribes, and that there are everywhere multitudes of children and young people — all these things sufficiently prove that for its own inhabitants the climate is a health-giving one. Respecting Europeans and all white men, the question becomes complicated with a multitude of facts outside of merely local conditions and influences. Changes of climatic conditions naturally call for adaptations of the physical system to meet the new requirements, the making of which may result either favorably or otherwise. In some cases chronic diseases may be effectually cured, or congenital morbific tendencies held in abeyance; in others the constitutional tendencies to some forms of disease may be quickened into fatal activity, or a latent liability to some unhealthy development, that at home might have remained dormant, may be hastened to its fatal termination. The differences of conditions between a residence in Europe or the United States and one in inter-tropical Africa are so very considerable, that a removal to the latter from the former must be somewhat perilous, even although the latter may be in fact quite as favorable to health and long life. In every case there must be a process of acclimatizing, which may or may not be attended by sickness, but is especially liable to be; and during that process, of three or six months, great care must be taken to avoid exposure to the direct rays of the sun, and to the night air, or any form of unnecessary physical or mental strain. The terrible force of the rays of the tropical sun is apt not to be properly appreciated and guarded against, and the night air, continuing well into the morning, is only a little less dangerous. High feeding, especially on animal food, must be avoided, and alcoholic drinks, even in the mildest forms, are superlatively evil. A wholesome and even generous diet, made up chiefly of farinaceous food, with vegetables and fruits, is desirable, with regular sufficiently-abundant sleep. With these things properly cared for, there is no reason to presume that the climate of Congo land is less healthful than our own more widely variable seasons.

In respect to its ethnology, Congo land is the home of the typical Negro. To the very partial observations to which these people have been submitted they appear to be substantially the same throughout; but it is quite possible that a more intimate acquaintance with them and their traditions will detect more or less of tribal differences. There appears also to be a remarkable uniformity in the mental conditions of the whole population, which is a low, but not the lowest, stage of barbarism. They practice the mechanical arts, of a rude kind, and to a small extent, and their agriculture, which is their principal industry, though of the most primitive kind, is extensive and remarkably productive. As they have no winters or other seasons of unproductiveness to provide for, they escape the horrors of starvation that sometimes desolate the homes of more northern savages. The physical appearance of the people indicates the use of an abundance of food, which is also corroborated by the multitudes of children and the populousness of the country. Animal life is indeed decidedly sturdy and relatively wholesome, despite the many and great drawbacks that are inseparable from the conditions of barbarism. Politically, the people are divided into small tribes, each having its chief or "king," who rules without any clearly defined laws, though the "customs" are recognized and somewhat respected. On some occasions several of these "head men" and their retainers form temporary confederations for aggression or defense, but these are only partial and temporary. A large portion of the population are slaves, for any man may become a slave-holder by purchase or the spoils of war, but the condition of the slaves is not much less favorable than that of the nominally free. Polygamy is practiced without any legal restrictions, and a man's greatness is often measured by the number of his wives, and of course women are universally the property of their husbands.

Their religious ideas are the simplest and the grossest. They have no idea of God, a supreme, super-mundane, and a spiritual Ruler; neither have they any ethical code. Conscience with them is apparently only an undeveloped potentiality, and instead of the stoic's sense of honor they display only the coarsest forms of egotism, and self-respect is replaced by supercilious vanity. Their superstition is manifested at every point. They recognize the preternatural in every thing, and of course they are universally fetich worshippers. They believe in the future state, which is, according to their conceptions, very much like the present, and like most other savages they seek to provide for that state by offerings of whatever is most valuable at the grave, or to the *manes* of the dead. As the Greeks sacrificed a man's slaves to accompany and serve him in the spirit world, and as the Hindu widow was burned upon the same funeral pile with the body of her dead husband, that the outgoing soul might be duly attended, so the Congo chief is supposed to be accompanied by his retinue of slaves which are slain at his funeral. Mr. Stanley tells of a case where "a long ago superannuated potentate" had died, and the whole region was searched over for the purchase of slaves to be murdered at his funeral; and at length the sickening massacre was witnessed by two European traders, who were powerless to prevent the horrible transaction. It is enough to say respecting the morality of these Congoese, that they are heathens and barbarians, having, in the usual degree, the vices that universally prevail in such a state of society, with a corresponding absence of positive virtues. Though overbearing to inferiors, they are not brave, and therefore not greatly addicted to war-making; but, when out of danger, they are cruel, truculent, and altogether treacherous. They recognize white men as essentially a superior race of beings, to whom they readily give their confidence, and to individuals of whom attachments are sometimes formed not unlike that of a dog for his master; and through this influence it may doubtless happen that a genuine moral character may be evoked. By that mode of access the Christian teacher may be enabled to reach the latent moral element in the minds of these people, and so lead them to a higher moral and religious status. Something of this kind seems to have occurred between Livingstone and some of his personal associates; but we find only the most remote approaches to anything of a like nature in the relations of Stanley to his Congoese.

The volumes now before us, as has already been suggested, come to the public somewhat in the form of a report of proceedings of a commission sent out under the auspices of the "Comite d'Etudes du Haut Congo," an association constituted expressly for the prosecution of explorations on that river, of which association King Leopold II. of Belgium was the chief patron, and Mr. Stanley was the managing agent for the work in Africa. This has since given place to "The International Association of the Congo," constituted early in the present year by the Berlin Conference, in which nearly all the principal powers of Europe were represented by their plenipotentiaries, and in which also the representatives of the United States took part, and whose character and designs are thus stated in the "Declaration" made to and by the Belgian government:

The International Association of the Congo declares by these presents, that, in virtue of treaties concluded with the legitimate sovereigns in the basin of the Congo and its tributaries, it has been ceded the sovereignty of vast territories, with the object of founding a free and independent State; that conventions define the frontiers of the territories of the association as regards those of France and Portugal, and that the frontiers of the Association are shown on the annexed map. . . . [A map attached to the "declaration."] That it assures to foreigners who settle in its territories the right to buy, sell, or lease ground and buildings situated thereon, to establish houses of business and trade (without duties or imposts), under the sole condition of obeying the laws. It undertakes, in addition, to accord no advantage to the citizens of (any) one nation, without immediately extending it to the citizens of all other nations, and to do all in its power to put down the slave trade.

All rivers, lakes, canals, and roads are to be open to the free commerce of all nations. "Wares, of whatever origin, imported under whatsoever flag, by sea or land, shall be subject to no other taxes than such as may be levied as fair compensation for expenditure in the interests of trade." This stipulation is guaranteed by all the powers represented at the Conference, which included the United States, and all the nations of Europe except Switzerland and Greece. It was also agreed "that all the powers, exercising sovereign rights or influence in the aforesaid territories, engage to watch over the preservation of the native tribes, to care for the improvement of their moral and material well-being, and to co-operate in the suppression of slavery, and especially of the slave-trade. They will protect and favor, without distinction of nationality or of worship, all religious institutions and enterprises, scientific or charitable schemes and organizations for the purpose of leading the natives to know and appreciate the advantages of civilization. Christian missionaries, scientists, and explorers, their associates and property, shall be the objects of special protection. Liberty of conscience and religious toleration are expressly guaranteed to natives, the nations, and foreigners. The free and public exercise of all forms of worship, and the right to build religious edifices,

THE VILLAGE BUILT BY THOSE WHO WERE CARING FOR LIVINGSTONE'S BODY.

BOSTON UNIVERSITY
COLLEGE OF LIBERAL ARTS
LIBRARY

and to organize missions belonging to all creeds, shall not be limited or fettered in any way whatsoever."

The "Free State" of Congo, as here described, appears to exist, in respect to its governmental authority, in an "Association" guaranteed by the chief governments of Europe. Its rights of dominion within its proper territory is professedly derived from its former "legitimate sovereigns," which may do well enough as a legal fiction, and as a device for obtaining the needed sovereignty without violence or the sacrifice of the good-will of the local "sovereigns."

The arrangement is good for all parties—a decided improvement upon the policy of seizure and spoliation that prevailed in this continent after its discovery. Treaties with savage races may mean much or little according to the good faith or otherwise that prevails in their formation and execution; in this case it may be hoped that the united influences of the higher morality of our times, and the mutual jealousies of the "powers," will avail to protect the "Free State of Congo" from spoliation by any one of them, and that private enterprise and Christian philantrophy will here find a free field. The arena is ample, and its possibilities beyond estimate; its proper occupation and improvement will constitute the grandest bequest made by the closing to the incoming century.

MEANS OF SELF SUPPORT.

In respect to the industrial and commercial capabilities of this vast region it is very easy to err in either direction. No nation or people can purchase foreign wares beyond the value of what they have to sell, and it is too obvious to require proof that barbarians and savages are always poor. But the sources of wealth in all this region are both abundant and easy to be made available. The Congo has long been known as a channel for bringing ivory to the coast; and though much that could be gathered up from the remains of dead animals has been already marketed, still much of the same kind remains to be gathered. But the chief supply must be obtained by hunting and destroying the living animals. It is estimated that there are not less than 200,000 living elephants within the Congo basin, carrying in their heads an average of fifty pounds of ivory, of an aggregate value of $25,000,000. Among other forms of non-agricultural wealth may be named the skins of monkeys, goats, antelopes, buffaloes, lions, and leopards; the gorgeous feathers of tropical birds; the teeth of the hippopotamus; tortoise-shell, bees-wax, frankincense, and myrrh. Of the industries of the forests, those of palm-oil and India rubber are the principal, and of these the supply is practically unlimited, and they are rendered available by only a little comparatively unskilled labor. There are also vast sources of wealth in gum, copal, and orchilla weed, which may be picked up by all who will do so, and also in the camwood and redwood powder, which any woman may prepare for market. There are also large opportunities for the production of the metals by native artisans, who now operate mines of iron, copper, and plumbago; nor is there any lack of gold, though not much has been done toward its development.

The agricultural productions of the whole region are already very considerable, with the possibilities of indefinite increase. "Every native village on the Upper Congo," writes Stanley, "has its sugarcane plots and maize. Bananas and plantains thrive marvellously. In the Kwa valley the natives eat bread of millet flour; but the cassava or manioc furnishes the staple of farinaceous food of the people along the main river."

A black field pea, that grows prolifically with but little cultivation, is much in favor, and of vegetables there are unlimited supplies of sweet potatoes, yams, cucumbers, melons, pumpkins and tomatoes; and many of the chief varieties of European garden and field plants are found to take kindly to the soil and climate, and to produce abundantly. Rice has been introduced by the Arabs in the eastern portion of the basin, and also wheat; and all the fruits of the torrid zone and many of more temperate regions are found to flourish luxuriantly. In the three great staples of sugar, rice, and cotton the capabilities of this region seem to be practically unlimited; but these can be effectually realized by the industry of the people — and industry is not a characteristic of barbarians, under a tropical sun, with an easily available natural supply for their few and simple wants.

The favorable solution of the African question depends very largely on the further question, whether or not the listless carelessness of the natives can be so far overcome as to enable them to develop the resources of the land about them; nor is this entirely hopeless. Already all along the chief rivers the pursuits of trade are overcoming the natural indolence of the chiefs and of other unofficial traders; and the twin passions, avarice and love of display, are producing their natural results in the form of productive industry. It has been demonstrated that the natives will work for wages, and also that the presence of foreign wares awakens an earnest desire for their possession. If, therefore, these people shall indeed be effectually restrained from war, and the slave trade and slavery be rooted out, the chiefs will have only the pursuits of trade and industry for their occupation; and with the increase of wealth will come also increased wants, which will in time call for increased productions. And if it shall be provided for in the regulations of the International Association, all intoxicating liquors shall be effectually excluded, there would seem to be room to hope that the material civilization and elevation of Congo land is not to be despaired of. No doubt, however, the most formidable difficulty in the case will be found in the incompetency of the white men who will be called to aid in the execution of the work. The pages of the work before us show very clearly how grievously the one responsible head of the enterprise found himself handicapped by the incompetence, the indolence, and the perverseness of his appointed assistants. Men go on such expeditions without any adequate conception of their requirements; they are heroes at home, but utterly fail in times of trial. Others are mere adventurers or romancers, who have no relish for steady and taxing labors; or, worse still, some are both selfish and vicious, and will hinder where they are expected to help. If failure shall come to the enterprise, these will be its procurers.

A GREAT MISSION FIELD.

Probably the question of the most lively interest with many of our readers will relate to the possibilities of this vast region as a field for Christian missions. The three great conditions to be taken into account in choosing a field for evangelistic propagandism — sufficient breadth, accessibility, and probable permanence of the people — are found here in all needed fullness. Within this field is found a large share of one of the great ethnic divisions of the human race — less numerous than no other race except only the Chinese and the Hindus — freely offered to the Christian enterprise of the age, and destined beyond any reasonable peradventure soon to become civilized. And in respect to the conditions that promise growth and expansion of the population, instead of the diminution and decay that have so often among barbarous nations resulted from the processes of civilization, here is all that can be wished. There is indeed no reason to apprehend that the cases of the American Indians and the South Sea Islanders, in decadence along with enlightenment, will be repeated among the natives of the Congo land; and unless all visible indications shall prove fallacious, the Negro is the coming man. These primary conditions therefore are all that could be desired, and the Christian heroism of the age is challenged by them to enter in and possess the land.

It would, however, be a great mistake to assume that an easy conquest is here promised; for though the obstacles to be overcome are largely negative in character, yet are they both real and formidable. The absence of religious convictions and institutions among the people offers very small advantages if there is also a corresponding want of religious susceptibilities. The obstacles to be overcome are chiefly the all-pervading mental and social inertia—the almost absolutely universal indifference in respect to every thing beyond material interests and sensuous pleasures. Heathenism is practically the synonym of depravity, which is both negatively and positively antagonistic to Christian truth and the wholesome restraints of the Gospel. Nor can there be, in even the least compacted tribal or personal relations, an entire absence of social influences; and these will always co-operate with the prevalent tendencies of the common characteristics. The superstition that is always so effective in the heathen mind, while as the expression of the religious intuitions and instincts of the soul it offers a way of access for religious instruction—just as St. Paul used Athenian "extreme religiousness" as a means by which to teach the highest and purest theism—nevertheless at once indisposes the mind to wholesome instruction, and also cherishes its own vanities in opposition to the pure and lofty doctrines and precepts of Christianity. As in the individual soul the successful operations of the Gospel are always effected against opposition, and appear in the form of a victory, so must the Gospel in its approaches to nations and peoples attain to success only by overcoming. The fact that a people are without letters, and have only the faintest ethnic traditions, and are almost entirely destitute of both social and religious institutions, while it may indicate the probability of but little positive and organized opposition to the Gospel, shows however that a great amount of severe and long-continued labor will be required in order to insure success.

The methods of practical operations in Christian teaching must of course be adapted to local conditions and peculiarities. Religious observances and institutions very largely receive their forms from their environments, as indeed should be the case; and it is great unwisdom to attempt to transplant and reproduce the outgrowths of local conditions into places and among peoples with whom the conditions that first originated them are wanting. Foreign missionaries have very much to learn and unlearn along this line; since, in all cases, the methods of evangelistic action, and the resultant religious and ecclesiastical institutions, must be adapted to the requirements of their circumstances. The "Articles of Religion" of the Methodist Episcopal Church, made up of fragmentary excerpts from the "Thirty-nine Articles" of the Church of England, were from the first a wholly inadequate and ill-expressed formulary of Christian doctrine, because they were originally designed for other and widely different conditions from those of the pioneers of American Methodism. The attempt to make them the standards of faith for Hindus, and Chinese, and Japanese, is therefore, simply the perfection of absurdity. So, too, our "General Rules," because they were originally prepared for and adapted to a very widely different order of things from anything now found among us, have become, even at home, thoroughly obsolete and without meaning; and certainly only the most insensate literalistic traditionalism would think of setting them up as the ethical code of those to whom the things referred to are wholly unknown. And so in attempting to propagate the Christian faith along the Congo, and to establish religious practices and institutions, it will be well to carefully discriminate between what in our home religion is essential to Christianity and what is only incidental, to be used or laid aside as may seem to be expedient.

It will probably be found that even the divinely appointed institution of "preaching," according to the usual acceptation of that term, will be found not the best suited for Christian instruction among the heathen tribes of Congo land. The work must begin very much lower down than the conditions of mental and social life that are supposed to exist where public address is an available form of teaching. The process by which those heathen barbarians are to be Christianized must provide for their mental elevation as necessary to their acceptance and retention of the saving lessons of the Gospel. It must, therefore, begin with the personal influence, made effective principally by examples, of the missionary among the people. He must, therefore, reside sufficiently near to them to be known and felt by them, which means practically that there shall be missionary stations provided with all the conditions of home life, so affording opportunities for informal oral instruction, the creation of a written language, and especially the instruction of the children.

As in the occupation of the country for its industrial development, it has been judged necessary to establish stations at proper points, with the required buildings for residences and storehouses, and to plant gardens and provide, as far as practicable, for self-sustentation, so, and even more largely, must missionary work be carried on by the slow but sure processes of occupation and permanent residence. The theory of self-support, though easily rendered absurd and impracticable by its too exclusive application, is no doubt the only theory upon which missions in interior Africa can be successfully prosecuted. Transportation and outfit and temporary sustentation must, of course, be provided in advance; but after the field has been reached and the station provided, mother earth and the strong right arm of the missionary, with such help as he may employ, wielded with cheerful force and sustained by a brave heart, must be the chief dependence. The practicability of this method has been tried by both the Livingstone Congo mission, which has recently been placed under the patronage and guardianship of the American Baptists, and by the English Baptist missions; and, to some extent, similar methods of missionary work are now carried on in various parts of the African continent. Mr. Stanley, though evidently friendly, never assumes the role of the advocate of the missionaries or their work; but occasional glances are now and then given by him, which are all the more valuable because they are purely incidental. We give the annexed as a specimen, and also as an illustration, of what an African missionary station may be:

"A few miles beyond, we begin the descent into the broad valley of Lukamga, where we are hospitably received by Mr. and Mrs. Ingham, of the Livingstone mission. * * * The mission cottage was as dainty within as any residence need be. A spacious garden behind it presented a vivid promise; a well-kept court or plaza in front was surrounded by store-rooms, kitchen and schoolrooms. Under the shadowy caves were to be seen the mission children, with their subdued air, as though they were impressed with the awful mysteries of the alphabet. It rather encouraged me to believe that the Congo climate, even in that low hollow of Lukamga, was endurable, when I here saw a delicate-looking lady bear herself so bravely. * * * My sojourn of twenty-four hours was enjoyed with the most exquisite pleasure. Ten men might have utterly stripped and carried away the veneer of civilization on that mission-house, and left it bare and barbarous (it probably cost only £100); but the art was in the lady's hand's, and the rich gift of taste inherited in far away England had diffused attractiveness over the humble home."

Another remark of our author, made in another case, and without any intended reference to the missionary work, is highly suggestive. Estimating the probable number of elephants in the whole country, he drops the remark: "Mr. Ingham, a missionary, lately shot twenty-five elephants, and obtained money for the ivory," which he elsewhere estimates at more than a hundred dollars for each animal. This seems very much like "self-support," achieved without any neglect of real missionary duty.

But all this implies the important consideration that to do successful missionary service in Africa a man must have the elements of character that insure success from the start. He should, of course, have a thoroughly sound physique, with large powers of endurance; but above all else he should have a brave heart and a cool head. A moderate share of enthusiasm may not be without its value, but there should be not a spark of fanaticism. Deep religiousness of character is doubly needful—first, to qualify him to preach Christ in every word and action, unconsciously as well as of set purpose; and, next, to sustain his spirit among the discouragements that are sure to come upon him, and to cause him to feel that it is his highest privilege to labor and suffer for Christ: and only second to this is a buoyancy of animal spirit—the very soul of cheerfulness and hopefulness among adversities. The successful African missionary goes thither to live and to work for the Master rather than to die; and accordingly he is careful not to expose his health to unnecessary perils, and also to be doing something whenever possible—the small things as well as the great—not accounting any service beneath him. The work of the true missionary must be a "labor of love;" and that this may not fail of its reward it must be sustained by "the patience of hope," never despising "the day of small things."

To attempt a mission in the Congo, there should be a company of half a dozen strong, young or middle-aged stalwart and common-sense men. There should be neither woman nor child in the first expedition, though at a later stage of the work the presence of the right kind of women is well-nigh a necessity. And above all else, there should be no fine gentlemen. Every missionary to Africa should be a man of faith, who believes in the divinity of his calling, and also in *quinine* as the *magnum donum Dei*, through the instrumentality of which he is to accomplish his mission—just the opposite of the fanatic, who tempts God by exposing himself to uncalled-for perils. That there are such men in the churches we will not doubt; but how they may be found out and brought to the front and initated into the work is a matter much more difficult to settle.

The Methodist Episcopal Church has two distinct missions in Africa, both under a common superintendency: one in Liberia, which has been very carefully administered for half a century, with only moderate results; the other just now in its incipiency, led by Bishop Taylor, and designed to reach from ocean to ocean, through Angola and the valley of the Zambezi, south of the Congo basin. Of the former of these nothing now needs to be said, since it is not an aggressive body, and especially not a mission to heathen Africa. Of the latter, it is yet too soon to speak of results, but we are free to utter words of decided commendation in respect to the theory upon which it is projected; to wit, that after the missionaries shall be established in their proper stations, and fairly engaged in their work, they are expected to provide, as far as possible, for their own maintenance, which we see no reason to doubt is wholly practicable. The three or four zealous and godly persons in the expedition who, misinterpreting the divine promises, expected to be preserved by miracles instead of by the use of the natural methods that God has provided, have also emphasized their folly, and perhaps set a limit to that form of fanaticism; and if so, the life that has been sacrificed has not been wholly thrown away. The survivors have learned that God saves by means, and that, having the means of safety at hand, it is neither faith nor piety, but presumption, to tempt God by refusing to use them. But should the greater part of Bishop Taylor's heroic band succumb in death, or hasten their flight homeward, we shall still expect that a good work will be done by those who continue in it with those who shall hereafter join them, and that the wilderness of the Zambezi valley shall yet bud and blossom, and bring forth its rich fruitage for the Lord of the harvest.

And shall not our Church have a part in the the evangelization of the millions that sit in dark ness in all the vast area of the Congo basin? Have we not the men for this work — such men as we have described? and is there not the requisite enthusiasm, at once fervid and discreet, to lead them forth to a work so glorious? May it not be hoped that Stanley's Congo will act as a trumpet-call to the Church for Africa?

Yes, Dr. Curry, our church has the men and the women too, whose hearts are burning with holy fire and self-sacrifice, who are ready to obey the promptings of the Holy Ghost and adopt Africa as their home and live and die in that sin-cursed land. Twenty of them sailed from New York March the twentieth, and nine more, full of the Holy Ghost and faith, sailed for Africa Oct. 2, and others are ready to take their flight for the land they love, and go and tell the poor African that Jesus died to save him. God is raising them up on every side and sending in the money to meet all necessary expenses.

As Bishop Taylor is now establishing missions on the Congo river, the reader will be glad to know what Mr. Stanley says of the Congo region: "This territory has gold and silver deposits, abundance of copper and iron mines, great forests of priceless timbers, inexhaustive quantities of rubber, precious gums and spices, pepper and coffee, countless herds of cattle, immense supplies of ivory, and many other articles of commerce.

In this equatorial belt there are, perhaps, 90,000,000 of people, with chiefs, kings, republics, kingdoms and empires, much of the immense population is *tractable.* These nations are amiable enough, as far as we have experienced in the last six years, for all purposes of peaceful commerce up and down the main river and its affluents."

Very well, then if they are *amiable* enough for peaceful commerce then they are amiable enough for Christian missions, and it is well that missions *are being and shall be* established among these amiable people. Why should we fear to go among them in the name of the Lord and teach them the way of life? Why should the Christian minister fail to have as much zeal and self denial as the enterprising traveller and trader? Why do professed Christians cling to their relatives and hinder them from following the promptings of the Holy Ghost in going to Africa to administer the bread of life to these blood-bought people?

Some are afraid they will lose their lives among the natives. Hear what Mr. Stanley says, "I have journeyed 9,000 miles during the past six years and *my only weapon has been an umbrella.* I have been served a warm appreciation of our visits and a great desire for a continuation of our intercourse. My reception among the natives has been kindly, in most instances effusively enthusiastic." I hear that ye that are afraid of these people and will neither go yourself or let your loved ones go to teach them of Jesus. What account will you give at the day of judgment; will you be clear of the blood of souls?

I am happy to learn that the Postal Union is extended to this Congo State so that five cents will carry a letter from the United States to the Congo State and other mail matter will be carried either way at a cheap rate. Surely the world is moving! Mr. Stanley says "The natives are born traders. They will leave their homes for a market 500 miles away and will remain for months, patiently waiting for the coasting caravans."

See what enterprise they manifest and imagine

what they would do for Jesus if they only knew him and felt his love in their hearts. Who will go and tell them of Jesus and his love? It seems to me that Almighty God, Father, Son and Holy Ghost is crying out, "Whom shall we send and who will go for us?" Thank God that so many are responding, "Here am I, send me."

THE CONGO RIVER.

Henry M. Stanley gives the following graphic description of this vast water-way, "The Rhine? Why the Rhine, even in its most picturesque parts is only a microscopic miniature of the lower Congo. The Mississippi? The Congo is one and one-half times larger than the Mississippi and certainly from eight to ten times broader. You may take your choice of nearly a dozen channels and you will see more beautiful vegetation on the Congo than on the American river? The latter lacks the plains and the calamus, while the former has a dozen varities of the palm. Besides it possesses herds of hippotami, crocodiles innumerable; monkeys are gleefully romping on the islands and the main; elephants are standing sentry, like the twilight of the dark forests by the river-side; buffaloes, red and black, are grazing on the rich grass plains. There are flocks of ibis, black and white parrots, parroquets and guinea fowl. The Mississippi is a decent grayish colored stream, confined between two low banks, with here and there a town of frame houses and brick. The Congo is of a tea color on its left half and on its right half it is mainly chalky white. You take your choice, tea or milk, and as for the towns, I hope the all-gracious Providence will bless our labors and they will come bye and bye, meantime there is room enough and to spare to stow away the half of Europe comfortably upon its spacious borders. The Nile? Ask any of those gallant soldiers who have tugged their way along the Nile cataracts what they think of the Nile to spend a holiday upon. The Danube? Ah, it is not to be mentioned with the Congo for scenery. The Volga? Still worse. The Amazon? By no means. You will have to ascend very far up the Amazon before you will see anything approaching the Congo scenery.

Although the river is equal in volume to the Nile, Zambezi, and Niger together, it is utterly barren of classic associations. Neither roving ancients or wandering moderns of grand renown have visited this river. No grand event is connected with its name,

Nothing has been performed in connection with the Congo to make its history popularly interesting to those who are not engaged in commerce, or some special study of it. No history, novel, or scientific enterpirse of any magnitude is associated with it. It has a dismal local history that arouses a gruesome feeling when we recall the slave-trading period. Ships of war of many nations have ascended the river. They have anchored for a short time abreast of Boma, and then sailed away. British consuls and other European naval officers have visited Boma frequently, and some have ventured as far as the lowest of the Livingstone Falls.

In the gardens of Boma, some of the traders have distinguished themselves as horticulturers. Oranges, citron, limes, papaws, guavas, and pine-apple are among the fruits obtainable in the seasons. European sweet potatoes, onions, turnips, lettuce, cabbage, and beans thrive sufficiently

CANOE BUILDING BY HENRY M. STANLEY.

BOSTON UNIVERSITY
COLLEGE OF LIBERAL ARTS
LIBRARY

well. Fresh meat from bullock, sheep, goat, and fowls, including ducks may be obtained, so that with rice, wheaten bread, and the help of a good cook, a European has no reason to regret Congo life, providing *discretion governs his conduct regarding his diet, and cold draughts are avoided.*

POSSIBILITIES OF COMMERCE ON THE CONGO RIVER.

The Manhcester people, of England, are enquiring "What can the natives of Africa give in exchange for our cloth?" Mr. Stanley replies, "If sailing ships and steamers can be sent to the upper Congo basin by the Manchester people, they will obtain three times, at least, more of West African produce than they obtain from the whole of the West African coast, extending from Gambia to St. Paul de Loando, or £50,000,000 worth of produce. Since they cannot send sailing or steam vessels, they must build two sections of narrow gauge railroad respectively, fifty-two and ninety-five miles in length, connected by steamboat navigation, or a connected railway 235 miles long, and they will obtain as much produce as such a railroad can convey from their trading agents on the upper Congo, who will collect it from over one million native Africans, who are waiting to be told what further produce is needed beyond ivory, palm oil, palm kernels, ground nuts, gum, copals, orchilla-weed, cam-wood, cola nuts, gum tragacanth, myrrh, frankincense, furs, skins, hides, feathers, copper, india-rubber, fibre of grasses, beeswax, bark-cloth, nutmeg, ginger, castor-oil, etc. Mr. Stanley says that if this railroad was built, the traffic would be so great as to make more than 400 tons per day which at one penny per ton per mile would make a revenue for freight only £152,000, which with the freight going into the interior would make the yearly revenue about £300,000, exclusive of passengers.

How long will it be before such a railroad is built that has such a prospect of becoming a source of income on the millions of pounds that are waiting for some profitable investment?

When commerce has opened this railroad, how easy it will be for the missionaries to reach the interior. What a vast saving of time and money and precious lives?

CHAPTER III.

H. M. STANLEY'S EXPERIENCE AND OBSERVATIONS.

As Bishop Wm. Taylor is planting stations on this mighty river and expects to call for many missionaries for this purpose, and as many travellers and traders will be found there, it will be well for all concerned to mark well the following remarks of Mr. Stanley. A careful attention to these rules, by all concerned, will not only preserve precious lives, but it will tend to increase both health and bodily comfort. As to the heat of the climate of the Congo, he observes: "The mean of the highest observation of temperature is only 90 degrees, while the mean of the lowest is only 75. Clad in clothes suitable for work, a European could perform as much work on the Congo as he could in England, provided a roof or awning was over his head. The heat of the sun, on a clear day rises from 100° to 115°, which is naturally dangerous if a person stand still, and exposes himself to its influence. On the march it is not to be feared for its immediate fatal results. But though not immediate, it excites violent perspiration, consequent prostration, and loss of energy, little likely to be recuperated rapidly in a new country like the Congo.

Hence in all my African travels I have confined my marches to the early morning between 6 and 11 A. M.

For three months of the year it is *positively cold*, and during the rest of the year, there is so much cloud and the heat is so tempered by the South Atlantic breezes, that we seldom suffer from its intensity. After a rain storm which has cleared the atmosphere, exposure to the direct force of the sun's heat would soon prove the power of the equatorial sun. The nights are cool, sometimes *even cold*, and a blanket is, after a short time, felt to be indispensable for comfort.

At the stations, missions, or factories, there is no necessity for exposure; a double thickness to the umbrella affords ample covering, and there are few localities where the shade of a tree is not conveniently near, while superintending the outdoor work. European artisans should not be compelled to expose themselves, except on rare occasions; but no precautions can be too great if they prevent sun strokes. The sun is the only real enemy to the European. To raise a safe protection against its malign influence is always possible, though seldom practiced. The factory clerk's position is the safest. The missionary ought also to be safe; but before he arrives at his destination he has generally strained his strength by insane pedestrian exercise, and the explorations of deep grassy tunnels, to which the heat of the Turkish bath bears no comparison. In one day's march, too, he has several times filled his stomach with cold water, and has undergone numerous transitions and variations of temperature, the mean of which may amount to 40 degrees Fahrenheit.

When the body is at rest the perspiration is imperceptible, but violent exercise and all powerful action under the direct action of the sun, soon force copious perspiration. In itself this might not be dangerous. The danger is incurred when hastening for relief and coolness, the shade of a tree or a veranda is sought, and the heedless exposure to the cold wind *chills the clothing, and body suddenly*, effectually closing the pores of the skin, to the vital derangement of the system. Immunity from these derangements can easily be obtained by the resident of a station or mission by keeping the temperature of the body as equable as possible.

It is the inequality of the climate of the Congo that must be guarded against. If the resident pays less attention to malaria and miasma, and devotes himself more to the study of preserving his system against the pernicious influences of these excessive variations of temperature, he need entertain but little fear of the Congo. A book might be written illustrative of this one fact.

While I do not deny that there is a certain quantity of miasma in the air, my belief is that it was the least of the evils from which the members of our expedition suffered. At Banana and Boma, in the midst of marshy exhalations, situated almost at the waters edge, the Europeans have enjoyed better health than our people at Vivi, on that singular rock platform 340 feet above the river. Almost complete immunity from sickness has been enjoyed at Kinshassa, just ten feet above high water. At Equator Station, with a river only five feet below its foundations, creeks, sable as ink surrounding it, the ground unctious with black fat alluvium, Europeans enjoy better health than at Manyanga, 240 feet above the river, and 1100 feet above the sea. Fourteen miles away from Manyanga, and eight miles removed from the river, we have a station on the plains of Ngombi, 1500 feet above the sea, where our people have enjoyed better health than at Manganza Hill, 150 yards in diameter and ravines 200 feet deep are around it on all sides, except at the narrow neck thirty yards across. Banana Point—six degrees below the Equator—only five feet above the brackish waters of its creek, is proved to be much healthier than Sierra Leone, over eight degrees north of the Equator, which has been called "the white man's grave," despite the number of medical inspectors who have employed their best judgment and experience in endeavoring to modify the fatal influences that seem to surround the latter place.

On some men destined to do great deeds in the Congo state, these chapters on the climate will create a desire to protect themselves against these inequalities or variations of temperature. On others destined to be failures, either to return, and rail ignorantly against they know not what, or to enrich the already fertile soil of Congo land with their bodies, they will have no effect."

A WORD TO THE DOCTORS.

Our doctors would do well to study what are the best foods required by those who live in the tropics. A fertile physiological field for exploration and discovery lies in this direction. Personally I would wish to impress a few things upon the mind of the medical explorer as they relate to those "other causes deleterious to health."

He advises abstinance from intoxicating drinks. The moderate use of tea and coffee he recommends. Palm wine exercises a dangerous effect upon the kidneys and stomach, unless taken when perfectly fresh. Potted sardines and yellow salmon provoke the appetite but suggest biliousness. All that is left that may be said to be perfectly safe is limited in the extreme—home-made bread, rice, a few vegetables, fruit and condensed milk.

Some harmless, mild liquid is needed which is agreeable and palatable, uninebriating as tea and as inoffensive to the stomach as milk, which neither affects the nerves nor kidneys, and is a portable food, easily assimilated by the digestive organs. Until some earnest physiological student can assist our deficiencies, I propose the following simple rules to be observed by those to whom the preservation of their lives has some interest.

BUILDING STATIONS.

1. Never build in a gorge, valley, ravine or any deep depression of land, that may serve as a channel for collecting wind currents. A free diffusion of air is required in your surroundings. The nearest points to the sea, plains, extended plateaus, as far removed as possible from any dominating superior heights that would cause irregular air-currents, are the safest localities. The lower story should be clear of the ground, unless you have made the floor imporous by cement or asphalt. In the grassy plain the floor of your living room should be at least twelve feet above the ground.

2. Avoid unnecessary exposure to the sun.

3. Guard against the fog, dews, and chills of evening, night and early morning.

4. Let your diet be as good as your circumstances will permit, but be prudent in your choice. Butter, cheese, and dishes swimming in oleaginous matter, are unsuitable to the conditions of the climate. Roasted ground nuts are a mistake. Always reject the fat of meats on your plate, all fats cause bile, rancidity and nausea, in the tropics. Never begin the day with an early meal of meats. Bread made at the station is better than biscuit. At 11 A. M. cease work and eat your dinner of meats, fish, vegetables, dry bread, and weak black tea with condensed milk. At 1.30 proceed to your work, and at 6.30 take your prudent supper of fish, fowl or meats, with vegetables, dry bread, rice, tapioca, sago and macaroni pudding. Amuse yourself with social conversation and reading till nine.

5. Sleep on blankets and cover up to your waist with a blanket, or woollens.

6. If marching, rise at 5 A. M., take lunch and be ready for the road by 5.30. Halt at 11 A. M. in mercy to yourself, your men and your animals, and do no more for the day. On halting, put on your wrapper to allow your body to *cool gradually*. Get under shelter as quick as you can if your camp is in an exposed position.

7. Observe the strictest temperance. Drop all thoughts of tonics. If you need tonics apply to a doctor. Your best tonic will be two grains of quinine.

8. If engaged in out-door work, never be in the sun without a strong, double umbrella; for head-dress have your choice of cork helmet, topee, or Congo cap.

9. If during the march you have been without an ample umbrella, a wetting need not be danger-

ous; but it becomes positively so, if after excessive perspiration, rain or an accident at the river crossing, you remain any time quiescent *without changing your clothes.*

10. When on the march the lighter you are clad the better, because at the halt you will need your wrapper or overcoat. Very light flannel will be sufficient for your dress, owing to the exercise you take. Light russet shoes for the feet; knickerbockers of light flannel; a loose light flannel shirt, a roll of flannel round the waist and a Congo cap for the head, will enable you to travel twelve miles a day without distress.

11. At the station, or mission, your clothing should be light, though not in the undress uniform of the road.

12. Do not bathe in cold water unless you are newly arrived from a temperate climate. The temperature of your bath is not safe below 85 deg. Let your bath be in the morning, or before dinner. The tepid bath is the most suitable.

13. Fruit should be eaten in the morning; oranges, mangoes, ripe bananas, guavas and papaws. Only the juice of the pineapple is to be recommended. *Never eat any fruit in the tropics at dinner.*

The same prudence that is required for protection against draughts, sudden chills, catarrh, bronchitis and pulmonary diseases in Europe, should be exercised, with the only difference that in the tropics the clothing should not be so heavy.

The diseases on the Congo are very simple, consisting of fevers and dysentery. The fevers are: 1. Common ague, less to be feared than an English cold. 2. The remittent fever, which is an exaggeration of the ague; this may last several days. 3. The pernicious bilious type, which is attended with serious complication and is more dangerous. This form may be altogether avoided by living wisely and well. Intoxicating drinks and tobacco are a damage. Dr. Martin gives the following rules: 1. Care in diet, clothing and exercise are more essential for health than medicine. 2. Observe strict temperance and moderate the heat by all possible means. 3. After the heat has predisposed the body, the sudden influence of cold has the most baleful influence. 4. The best way is to keep the body cool and avoid heating drinks. 5. The cold bath is death in the collapse that follows any great fatigue of body or mind. *Licentious indulgence* is far more dangerous and destructive than in Europe. 7. A large amount of animal food, instead of giving strength, heats the blood, renders the system feverish, and weakens the whole body. 8. Bread is one of the best articles of diet. Rice, split vetches are wholesome and nutritious. Vegetables are essential to good health, such as carrots, turnips, onions, native greens, etc. 9. Fruit, when sound and ripe, is beneficial instead of hurtful. 10. The same amount of stimulent, undiluted, is much more injurious than when mixed with water. 11. With ordinary precaution and attention to the common laws of hygiene, *Europeans may live as long at the tropics as elsewhere.*

Mr. Stanley goes on to say, "However well the European may endure the climate by wise self-government, years of constant high temperature assisted by the monotony and poverty of the diet, cannot be otherwise than enervating and depressing, although life may not be endangered. The physical force becomes debilitated by the heat, necessitating, after a few years, recuperation in a temperate climate."

Beyond what has been taught above, there is nothing in Congo land to daunt a man; indeed far less than in many parts of India, South America or the West Indies. My object in writing has been to prevent the silly fear of the climate. The above rules *if observed* will prevent at least three-fourths of the maladies that have punished our imprudent youths. Possibly the judicious will find reward in following their guidance as nearly as possible. The injudicious and unreflecting will also have their reward.

The mean highest temperature during the year 1882, at Vivi, was 90°, and the lowest during the same period was 67°; mean variation 25°.

Mr. Stanley says, " it is not Africa that *is* fatal, but the disregards of prudent considerations and most of all the use of high wines and spirits."

The territory of the New Congo State is almost half that of the United States. It has 400 miles of coast on the Atlantic Ocean and 5000 miles of navigable rivers and its agricultural and mineral wealth is almost boundless.

" The basin of the Upper Congo is one of great natural beauty and magnificence, as well as of immense and various resources. The superficial area drained by the Congo River system is 1,090,000 square miles, which are directly accessible on 5,250 miles of open and nagivable rivers — an enormous aggregate, which, by passing over one rapid, may be swelled to the yet higher total of over 6000 miles.

The population of the Nyam-Nyam country is about 370 to the square mile. Tippu Tib, the great Arab trader in the interior, who has traversed certain sections in the south-eastern portion, assured Stanley that he had passed through towns which it required two hours to traverse, and that the beauty of savannah, park, and prairie around them was indescribable. Stanley's estimate for the entire region of the Upper Congo places the population at 42,294,000."

Dr. Pogge and Lieutenant Weissman, who crossed the Upper Lubilast, write, "The country is densely populated and some of the villages are miles in length. They are clean, with commodious houses, shaded by oil-palms and bananas and surrounded by carefully divided fields, in which, quite contrary to the African practice, man is seen to till the soil while woman attends to the household duties.

From Lubilast to the Lumani, there stretches almost uninterruptedly a prairie region of great fertility, the future pasture grounds of the world. The reddish loam over-laying the granite, bears luxuriant grass and clumps of trees, and only the banks are densely wooded. The rain falls during eight months of the year from September to April, but they are not excessive. The temperature varies from 63 to 80 degrees. In the dry season it sometimes falls as low as 45 degrees.

A certain writer says: "The forests on the banks of the Congo are filled with precious redwood, lignum vitæ, mahogany, and fragrant gum trees. At their base may be found inexhaustible quantities of fossil gum, with which the carriages and furnitures of civilized countries are varnished; their boles exude myrrh and frankincense; their foliage is draped with orchilla weed, useful for dye. The redwood, when cut down, chipped and rasped, produces a deep crimson powder, giving a valuable coloring; the creepers which hang in festoons from tree to tree are generally those from which India rubber is produced (the best of which is worth two shillings per pound); the nuts of the oil palm give forth a butter, a staple article of commerce; while the fibre of others will make the best cordage. Among the wild shrubs are frequently found the coffee plant. In its plains, jungle, and swamp, luxuriate the elephants, whose teeth furnish ivory worth from eight shillings to eleven shillings per pound; its waters teem with numberless herds of hippopotami, whose tusks are also valuable; furs of the lion, leopard, monkey, otter; hides of antelope, buffalo, goat, cattle, etc., may also be obtained. But, what is of far more value, it possesses over 40,000,000 of moderately industrious and workable people, which the red Indians never were. And if we speak of prospective advantages and benefits to be derived from this late gift of nature, they are not much inferior in number or value to those of the well-developed Mississippi Valley. The copper of Lake Superior is rivalled by that of the Kwilu-Niadi Valley and of Bembe. Rice, cotton, tobacco, maize, coffee, sugar, and wheat would thrive equally well on the broad plains of the Congo. This is only known after the least superficial examination of a limited line which is not much over fifty miles wide. I have heard of gold and silver, but this statement requires further corroboration, and I am not disposed to touch upon what I do not personally know."

The whole large State is open to free trade for twenty years. It is also open for Christian missionaries. Let us rally to the will of Bishop Wm. Taylor till we can sing.

Another noble band of nine missionaries sailed from New York, for Africa Oct. 2, 1886, including Brother Arrundale and wife and son, of Baltimore, L. Fannie Cummings and Effie Brannua, of New England. They were full of faith and the Holy Ghost. Their testimonies at St. Paul's Church and at Mrs. Palmer's meeting were deeply impressive. While this book is being printed they are sailing down the coast of Africa. Most of them declared that they had adopted Africa as their home, where they are perfectly willing to spend their days and end their lives, so that they can have a part in the first resurrection with those that shall be redeemed from among the sons of Ham.

THE CONGO FOR CHRIST.

BY DAWSON BURNS, D. D.

Where Congo's wealth of waters rolls onward to the sea,
Where Afric's sons and daughters to idols bend the knee;
There treads the Christian herald, inspired by love and zeal,
And seeks, with life imperilled, the soul's immortal weal,

By forest, field, and village, round hills with hidden stores,
Through plains awaiting tillage, the lordly Congo pours;
And there in future ages, a countless host shall rise,
To follow saints and sages in triumph to the skies.

Not solitary floweth the Congo on its way,
But whereso'er it goeth, great streams their tribute pay;
So, to the rule of Jesus, shall all dominions yield,
And He whose suffering saves us, the sovereignty shall wield.

Each waterway ascended, let peace and commerce spread,
Till savage wars are ended, and slavery is dead;
And, man to man united, the living God shall find,
And, by his love incited, serve Him with child-like mind.

Where wends each mighty river, go forth, O Truth divine.
Imprisoned souls deliver, on clouded spirits shine;
Till Africa's dark races, from error shall be free,
And, raised to heavenly places, Christ shall their glory be.

CHAPTER IV.

BISHOP WILLIAM TAYLOR'S MISSIONS IN AFRICA.

Bishop William Taylor may well be called "*The apostle of self-supporting missions.*" Already he has planted these missions in India, where there is now a large and flourishing annual conference, which started under his labors in India in 1870. They are located in Calcutta, Bombay, Madras and in other central cities. Then, under the leadings of the Holy Ghost, he went to South America, and to save expenses, he went *steerage* passage, and when he got there he lived for two months on seventeen cents a day. Now we have flourishing stations, schools, colleges, and a university is in process of erection, which will be sufficient to furnish teachers for all the nations of South America. In 1884 the General Conference of the Methodist Church of Philadelphia, almost by acclamation, elected William Taylor, "Bishop of Africa," giving him a whole continent for his parish. His election and ordination were a marvel to many. The whole movement came upon the General Conference as an inspiration, and some are in doubt to this day, who made the nomination. None but a man of world-wide renown was worthy *of* or available *for* such an enterprise. But God had been preparing William Taylor for many years for this work; his faith had increased exceedingly, and his love abounded, and his courage was equal to the emergency. In the spirit of a true Apostle of the Lord Jesus he issued his call for volunteers to go to Africa — almost without purse or scrip — to go to Africa, to what part none knew at that time. To go to Africa on the self-supporting plan. To go without any opportunity to return, to be willing to labor and die for Jesus, in that far off unknown land. Men and women were soon offering themselves on every side, and as some of them had children and were not willing to break up their families, they took their children with them. Rev. A. E. Withey of Lynn, Mass., took his wife and four children, and they are all alive and well. William Mead of Underhill, Vermont, took a wife and six children, and they are all alive and well. Rev. Ross Taylor, the bishop's son, took his wife and four *small* children, and found he had made a mistake, owned it and returned to California, where he has been laboring with great success in revival work. Bishop Taylor started for England and Liberia Dec. 13, 1884. He visited the Liberian Conference and preached in Monrovia and other places until the Missionaries came along down the coast.

Fifty-two men, women and children sailed from New York for Africa on *The City of Montreal*, January 22, 1886. Singing in the face of mountain difficulties:

"The birds without barn or storehouse are fed;
From them let us learn to trust for our bread;
The saints what is fitting shall ne'er be denied,
So long as 'tis written the Lord will provide."

ON THE UPPER CONGO RIVER.

NEW MISSION STATION. 65

After a stormy passage they reached Liverpool, and had a happy greeting from the many friends of Bishop Taylor's mission in that city. Soon they sailed for Africa in the Steamer *Biaffra*. They had a delightful ride down the coast of Africa. Made many stops and observations. They sent home some beautiful letters. They had some very interesting religious meetings on board. On their way they found a trader, who lived at Mayumba, who wanted a missionary station there, and promised to support a missionary for one year. Bishop Taylor appointed Rev. A. W. Willis and wife, B. F. Northam and Carl Steedman, to commence a mission there. Mrs. Willis' health was poor from the beginning. Many trials awaited them. At length Mrs. Willis felt that duty called her to save her life by returning to the United States, and Mr. Willis started to conduct her home, but up the old Calaba river he took the African fever and died and was buried in the deep. Mrs. Willis reached the United States, and went at once to work for Jesus.

The Bishop met the missionaries at Cape Palmas, and they reached Loanda, March 19, 1885. For four long months they had their share of trials at Loanda. Most of them took the fever in some form. They had a large mansion for a home, with tents on the outside. Dr. Sumner went into the interior to spy out the best places for stations. The Bishop followed, after consulting with the Governor of that province for permission and for protection, and also for land to establish industrial schools; all of which were readily granted, and in time a station was established at Dondo, which is at the head of navigation on the Congo river and about 240 miles from Loando. Here Mrs. Dr. Myers Davenport and husband are stationed. She was a graduate of the medical department of the Boston Univerversity. Mr. Davenport is a teacher and very ingenious in many things. They have made this mission *self supporting already*, which is a great victory, they have an organ and are learning the people to sing as well as to pray. Dondo is a great centre of gathering for the caravans to and from the interior, and is a very important station. Fifty-one miles by foot path over the hills and mountains, along the banks of the Coanza river, is NHANGUEPEPO, the *receiving station* of Taylor's mission for Angola. Here Bishop Taylor and Brother Dodson dug a well. Here they have 2500 acres of land and an industrial school farm, with 200 banana trees and over 400 pineapple plants. Here Brother Dodson started a school under the fly of a tent and sat on a stool without legs, and taught the native children that sat upon the ground. Here mission buildings have been purchased and others have been built.

Rev. A. E. Withey writes: "We are wonderfully located for health, on an eminence overlooking fertile plains, which are surrounded by mountains, which one is never tired of looking at. We have cool breezes most of the day, comfortable nights and very few mosquitos. A half hour's walk brings us to the beautiful Coanza river, with its scenery. We have a comfortable stone house (the best in this section) have good herds of cattle, good flocks of sheep, goats and hens; tenderloin steak for four and a half cents a pound, pasturage for thousands of cattle; eggs six or nine cents a dozen, corn meal and mandioca flour three or four

SHANGUETEPO STATION.

**BOSTON UNIVERSITY
COLLEGE OF LIBERAL ARTS
LIBRARY**

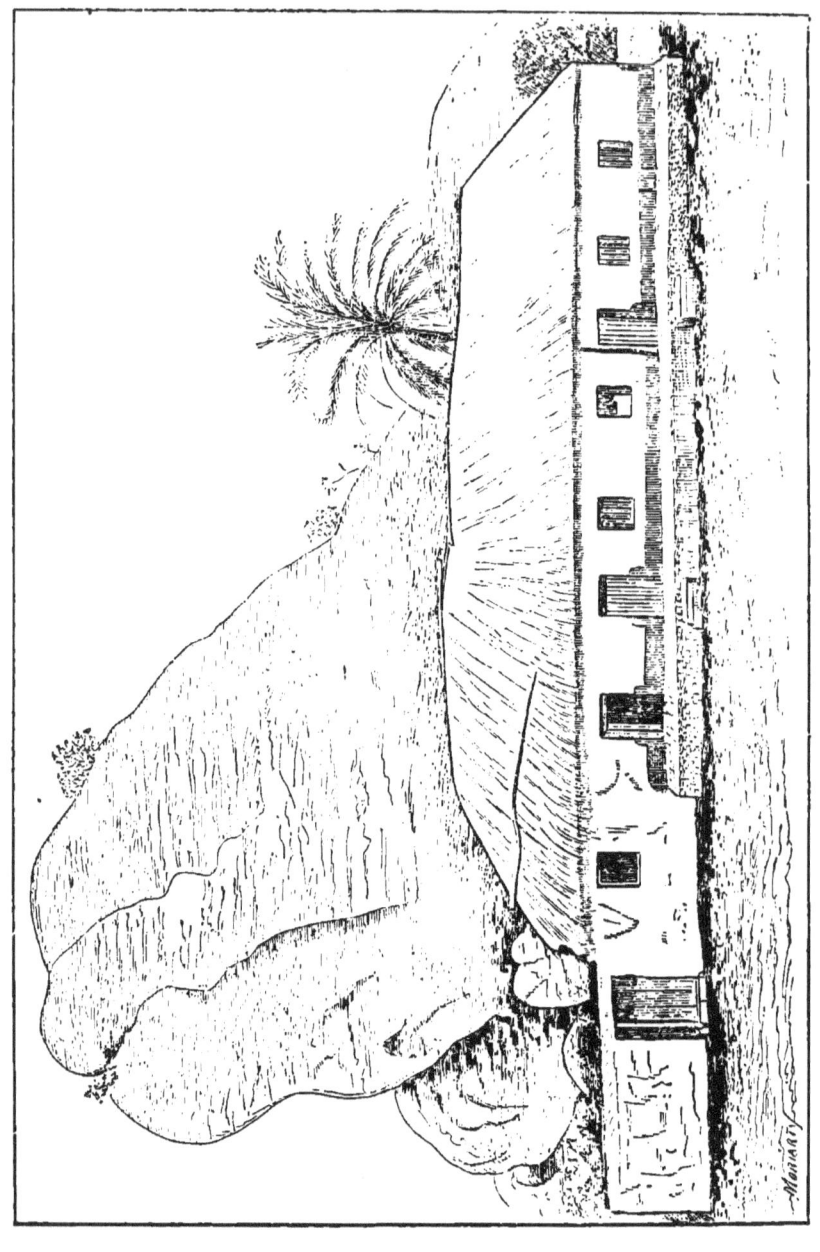

BISHOP TAYLOR'S MISSION AT PUNGO ANDONGO.

cents (in time of famine) about one-half cent in time of plenty. Bananas in their season, ten for a cent."

Pungo Andongo is the next station. It is thirty-seven miles across the rolling country from Nhanguepepo. Here we find stupendous cliffs of solid conglomerate of great variety and in great piles, with a passage through the centre over the rocks in to the middle, where there is a vast open space in which the village nestles. Dr. Livingstone speaks of this place as follows: "Pungo Andongo is situated in the midst of a group of curious columnar-shaped rocks, each of which is upwards of 300 feet in height. They are composed of conglomerate, made up of a great variety of rounded pieces in a matrix of dark red sandstone. They rest on a thick stratum of this rock.

These gigantic pillars have been formed by a current of the sea coming from S. S. E., and must have stood the surges of the ocean at a period of the world's history, when the relations of land and sea were totally different from what they are now, and long before the morning stars sang together, or the sons of God shouted for joy."

Here Rev. Joseph Wilkes and wife and daughter are stationed. Here a suitable set of buildings have been purchased; just exactly what the mission needs. Here a day and Sunday school have been started and a permanent station established. Brother Wilkes has opened a small store, and is thus helping to sustain himself and family. His wife has been very sick, but does not lay it to being in Africa. She is recovering, and all is well.

From Pungo Andongo you go through a woody country, with hills and vales, but no mountains, for sixty-two miles, when you reach MALANGE, on the eastern border of the province of Angola. Mr. Samuel Mead, Aida and Bertha Mead, Dr. Summers and Dr. Smith and family have gone there, and Dr. Summers has gone further into the interor to find suitable places for new stations. All these stations except Mambare are under the Portuguese government, so that the missionaries are well protected and well cared for.

In planting these stations the Bishop travelled on foot 600 miles and lost forty-one pounds of his former self, but since then he has visited England and various parts of Europe, regained his health and made up for his lost possessions.

When these women and children went out to Africa, there was a great company of false prophets that were sure " the women and children would all die and it was a fearful mistake to take them out into that barbarous land." But the fact is, the women have stood it better than the men and not one of them has died, and the children have stood it better than their parents, and are all alive and well. Mr. Charles Miller of Baltimore, was a young man of fine physique and bid fair for long life and service in the mission field, but when he was sick of African fever, he utterly refused to take the quinine to break it up; he persisted in saying, God would heal him by faith, but when he was too far gone he cried out for the medicine, but it was in vain. He died as the result. But he triumphed in Jesus as his mighty Saviour.

Bishop Taylor called for reinforcements this spring; twenty missionaries obeyed the call and sailed from New York March 20, 1886. The Bishop met them at Mayumba, and as the steamer made a long stop at KABINDA, near the mouth of the Congo river, Rev. J. L. Judson, an educated man from the South, who had been redeemed from slavery, and has great oratorical powers and some knowledge of medicine, this enterprising young man, with others went ashore and began to get acquainted with the people, and thought it would be a good place for a station.

The Bishop called a council, and it was decided to establish a station there, and Brother Judson was appointed superintendent, with Archie Steele and G. R. Thompson, assistants. After being there awhile he writes, "We are perfectly well in soul, and body, and spirit. I am proud to say we are succeeding admirably; the Lord is blessing everything we put our hands to, praise his holy name! We were kindly received by the Portuguese Governor, who treated us with distinguished respect, and rendered us assistance in transporting our effects from the beach, pitching our tents, etc. There are said to be a small number of towns in the radius of fifteen miles making an entire population of over half a million. This whole people have only one sermon a week, and that through an interpreter; have hardly heard of God or the Bible.

Alas, that there are rum factories here that exercise a most unwholesome influence on the morals of the natives! The rapidity with which we are acquiring the language, would astonish you; it cannot be otherwise, for we are with them all the time, advising, administering medicine and doing all we can to establish ourselves in their confidence."

After calling for more medicine and a medical cyclopœdia, he says: "There are no doctors in this country, and that to heal their bodies is the way to get into their good graces. I can take in return for medicine and advice, fowls, eggs, fruit and vegetables, which will help our supplies to hold out. I intend to commence building soon. I shall just have a spacious native house of Bamboo with a very large shed arrangement to take as many boys as I can well care for, and enter them on the industrial school plan for for five years. I have hundreds of applications for both boys and girls since I explained to them the nature of the work. It is a sad thing that we cannot have some ladies to take charge of the girls. The morals of the females are very low here, and the little girls should be cared for, and we cannot take them because we are unable to teach them sewing, house-keeping, washing, ironing and such things. A thousand ladies could be well employed in this Kabinda country. The people are teachable and willing to receive instruction, or advice of any kind. This is said to be the healthiest locality on the coast. The soil is very prolific, game is in plenty, such as quail, guinea fowl, pigeons and some large game."

From *The Presbyterian Observer:*—" One of the most remarkable men of the century is William Taylor, the Methodist 'Bishop for Africa.' He has begun two chains of missions across Africa, and hopes to start two more during the year. His missions are founded upon principles novel but sound. He enters into agreement with chief and people, agreeing on his part to import good preachers and teachers from the New World free of expense to the tribe, and to purchase tools and machinery for industrial schools. The chief and his people, on their part, are required to give a thousand acres of land for each school-farm; to clear and to plant, immediately, a few acres of the farm, to provide subsistence for the preachers and teachers ; to build houses for the workers, and to pay a small monthly fee for the tuition of day scholars. Boys and girls may work for their tuition. Those wishing a full course, must be allowed to remain in the school at least five years. By this agreement the natives are made to feel that they have made a valuable acquisition, and the mission is at once put upon a permanent, self-supporting basis."

The following letter is from Bishop Taylor, and shows the style of the man, who believes in hard work in the tropical climates to work off the fever :

"MAMBA, April 21, 1886.

I arrived here over a month ago. My man here is a fine young Frenchman, educated for a Roman Catholic priest, but was saved, and joined the Methodists six years ago, and has been for a few years an effective preacher. This station being in French territory, in which the schools are limited to the French language, we are masters of the situation in having this French brother. He was just recovering from an eight days' waste of fever when I arrived, but he turned in with me to clear and dig up and plant a field, and saw planks to floor our Mission house. So, for over a month, we have been hard at work in the sunshine from five to eight hours per day, putting in other hours in shade-work about the house. My Frenchman, Brother Benoit, is an indomitable and cheerful worker ; has become rugged and strong, and I never enjoyed better health in my life than in this work. I have to change my clothes, dripping wet with perspiration, twice per day. A Turkish bath is nothing compared with it. The British missionaries on the Congo (English) are forbidden to use axe or hoe, and last year six out of the fifteen of them died. My people in Angola work hard part of each day, and are all in good health. So, man's doom to eat bread by the sweat of his brow has a blessing under it. I expect to join my new party at Mayumba on the 15th of May, and proceed to the Congo. WILLIAM TAYLOR."

Bishop Taylor writes again:

"My plan, as you may know, is, first, to cultivate in profusion every thing required for food for all concerned; second, to cultivate yams, coffee, sugar, arrow-root, ginger, etc., that will in time bring us an income from foreign markets, and, as I said, the trading will grow in some places as one of our industries. I learn, by recent letters from Angola, that all our people are in good health, happy in their work, and making good progress in learning the Portuguese and the Menbundu languages."

Brother Benoit writes, "As the Bishop says, we have brought things to pass, and you will be better able to judge for yourself after I have given you the details of our work the last two months.

The first month we looked for a locality, cleared, digged, and planted sixteen rods of land in the valley. Every inch of ground was digged thoroughly, and we planted corn, sweet potatoes, yams, eddoes, and cassava, which is the staple food of the country. We also cleared in the bush an acre of land, cutting trees, etc. There we digged and planted another sixteen rods with about three thousand coffee seeds. We planted, also, eight rods in cassava. Then we planted fruit-trees

LEOPOLDVILLE STATION (NTAMO). STANLEY POOL.

BOSTON UNIVERSITY
COLLEGE OF LIBERAL ARTS
LIBRARY

and various other seeds. This finished the planting for the present. (I may here state that this was all done by the Bishop and myself. I had five natives working for five days, but as they were not efficient, I sent them away.) The Bishop is a wonderful man, indeed. He scored his sixty-fifth year on the second of this month of May, yet he worked these two months more and harder than myself, and he says his health was never better in his life. People at large in America can hardly believe, I suppose, that it is a Bishop of the Methodist Church that goes out to the field with an ax or a hoe to work in the soil under the hot rays of an African sun, on an average of six hours per day, yet is so,—Bishop William Taylor is thus sacrificing, in his old age, the rest and comforts which the many years of efficient service have earned him in his native land.

The last month the Bishop was with me, we sawed plank with a pit-saw. I knew nothing of this kind of work before. The Bishop told me the other day that it was not every young man that had learned to saw with a pit-saw under the tutorship of a Bishop of the Church. We put a floor, doors, and window-frames and casings, and also a a new roof on our house, and added a veranda all around. We built a house for the boys, and also a school-house, 20x40. We will be ready to begin school work soon.

There are many things we need here, such as tools and garden implements, and especially a boat, as we have to do all our travelling to the beach in canoes, and we are put to serious inconvenience. Whenever we receive goods from the steamer, they have to be brought up to this place by canoes or boats we may hire.

Bishop Taylor writes to *The Independent*, June 11: "I have supervision of the Liberia Annual Conference of the Methodist Episcopal Church, under the jurisdiction of the Methodist Episcopal Missionary Society, which has not fully reached the basis of self-support; but I will (D. V.) on my return to Liberia in a year hence, commence a line of self-supporting missions among heathen tribes in Liberia, to become purely self-supporting in the space of a year or a year and a half. My stations in South Central Africa commenced last year. After supplying my other stations I have nine men and one lady to accompany me to the Upper Congo and Kassai.

According to instruction from Leopold II, and the heads of the Congo State Government in Brussels, the Administrator-general here has given us a welcome, and will convey me, my party and all our freights to Mataddie, eighty miles from Banana, whence we will (D. V.) march by a narrow way over the Congo Mountains, 235 miles to Stanley Pool."

He writes again from "Banana, mouth of the Congo, June 11. I may remark in the premises, that the principle of self-support is simply the principle of equivalents in value that underlies all the commerce of the world. In the spread of the Gospel it appears under two forms. First, in the experience of a missionary pioneer going among the people who are not prepared to appreciate the Gospel or a Christian education as a value; and, therefore, to get a footing among them, he must build tents, or engage in other value-producing industry that will bring a return adequate to his support while he is laying the foundations of Christian life and organization, until there shall be a demand for and cheerful support of pastoral agency under the principle of direct exchange of equivalents. 'The laborer is worthy of his hire,' to be paid by those who share the benefits of his labors. 'They that preach the Gospel shall live by the Gospel' they preach. All my missionary workers in India and South America (about 150 men and women) are, and were from the first, supported by the people they serve on principle No. 2. A large majority of our workers in South Central Africa, now numbering — men, women and children — fifty-five, all in good health, and filled with love and zeal for God and His work, have to begin on principle No. 1; but the industries essential to the education of the rising generation of barbarous peoples will embrace, as legitimate part of our work, all the productive avocations necessary to the support of preachers, teachers and pupils. Success on this line is possible without any help from home; but to get a short cut on it we allow our friends in Christian countries to be sharers in the work by helping the brethren on their way, and providing the implements and machinery necessary to early working effectiveness. Together with this outfit the transit supply extends, not simply to passage to this dark land, but support for a year or two, till by prompt clearing, planting and cultivation, an adequate indigenous support can be obtained. Paying no salaries to agents at home, nor to workers abroad, the expense of this method of establishing self-supporting Missions is comparatively small."

Bishop Taylor writes from the Congo River: "We are going on the high line of human impossibilities, but have the fullest confidence in Him with whom all things are possible. The missionaries we have met belonging to the two societies operating on the Congo, the English Baptists and the Livingstone Inland, now belonging to the American Baptist Missionary Union, have given us an assuring welcome, and shown us great kindness. The Lord bless and reward them. He will. We arrived here at Stanley Pool, safe and sound on Friday morning, July 16th. We saw the chief of this district the same day, and everything clearly indicates that the King has come along in advance and marked out and prepared our way according to our expectation. We cannot anticipate Him, but probably He will have us start a base for a line of mission stations to be opened in the near future at Kimpoko, at the north-east corner of Stanley Pool, and at the junction of the Sankura and Kassai Rivers, about 409 miles from here. These are the two great strategetic points for work on the three greatest rivers of South Central Africa, the Congo, Kassai and Sankura, the two latter but recently explored, are of equal size, and both together greater than the Congo, above the Kwa mouth, or junction of the Congo and Kassai.

We are going in with Jesus Christ, the King, to do business on a scale somewhat commensurate with the demands of the perishing nations of Africa: and the available supply of infinite love and mercy. We go on immediately to Kimpoko, (D. V.) and commence work, and hope for the arrival of the rest of our party in a week or ten days. I expect that our friends and patrons in America and England will stand by us and work with God in providing all the money, and all the men and women from home that the King may require, for the accomplishment of the stupendous undertaking we have in hand. Glory to God in the Highest, peace on earth and good-will to the oppressed peoples of Africa. Amen.

     Your brother, WM. TAYLOR.

AFRICA'S CALL.
Tune, "Hallelujah, 'tis done!"
BY REV. ALEXANDER BLACKBURN.

Ethiopia's hands are stretched out unto God,
As they plead for the land where their forefathers trod.

Chorus.

Of our Jesus we'll sing, and our offerings we'll bring
Till Old Africa crowns him Redeemer and King.

In the blackness of sin they are waiting for light,
But the stains of their guilt Jesus' blood will wash white.

Though our fathers were slaves, now in Christ we are free,
And our brothers must know this same sweet liberty.

We will gird for the work, with our hearts full of love,
While we ask for that strength that comes down from above.

O our God, who led slaves out of Egypt, of old,
Bring forth now to freedom these millions untold!

O our Saviour, we pray that the cross Simon bore
May be known in his land, from its centre to shore!

O thou blest Holy Ghost, whom the eunuch received,
Plead for Afric's dark children, till all have believed!

Then at last, when we stand happy heirs with the Son,
All redeemed by his blood, and all nations made one,—

Chorus, last verse.

In full chorus we'll sing, and our loud praises bring,
Unto him who hath saved us, our Jesus, our King.

CHAPTER V.

Bishop Taylor is establishing industrial farms and proposes to learn the natives how to do various kinds of work. The following will show what can be done in this direction:

"Rev. W. C. Wilcox has tried the experiment of cultivating a considerable tract of land in order to draw a greater number of the native youths into his more immediate care, and so far the plan seems to be working successfully. These young people have proved unusually bright and tractable; they conform to the rules readily, acquire manual arts with great facility, and make rapid progress in learning to read and to write. In one of these schools a young man, six weeks after he had learned the letters of the alphabet, was able to set type, and within six weeks more he could both set and distribute type, correct proof, and print with commendable accuracy. Another learned the mason's art with equal facility, and a third the tailor's art. But, best of all, at all the stations they soon seemed to understand the gospel and to feel its claims on them and personally to yield themselves to the Saviour."

This was on the east coast of Africa and among the Congregational missions.

I called on Dr. Murdock of the Baptist mission rooms, in Boston, from whom I gather the following glorious facts:

Mission labor has been performed at Banza Manteke for seven years, and the Scriptures have been translated, in part, and circulated among the people, and they have been instructed in divine things. Some time this year the missionaries began to labor directly for the salvation of the people.

A man and his wife were converted. This gave the missionaries courage. They began to plead with God to pour out his Spirit in mighty power.

Rev. Mr. Richards writes: "I have continued to study hard, work earnestly, and pray believingly. For some time I have been praying for a more complete consecration,—to be filled with the Holy Spirit, and power for service, and for the Pentecostal outpouring of the Holy Spirit on the people. The bones that had been shaking for some time past began to stand up and show very evident signs of life. Truly the Pentecostal power came as I have never seen before; for the people began to bring out their idols for us to burn, and cry, "What must we do to be saved?" There was much opposition and persecution, which only seemed to increase the spiritual power; for the bitterest enemies and the greatest sinners were brought under the conviction of sin. The interest increased, and the people came up in large numbers to the station. The house became too strait and we were obliged to hold the services in the open air, and have continued to do so up to the present time; and we have more than seven hundred converts. The glorious fact is this, that Banza Manteke is no longer a heathen country, but more Christian than any I am acquainted with. I have had scarcely time to eat; for, from morning till night, I have been busy preaching, receiving inquirers, and treating the sick."

Later news has been received which proclaims the fact that more than a thousand have been converted; 850 of them adults or youths; the rest are children, and they give good evidence of the genuineness of the work of God upon their hearts. The work is spreading into the regions around. Indeed this has become an evangelizing centre of great power. "Glory be to the Father, and to the Son and to the Holy Ghost!" And let all the people say, Amen. This wonderful work of God is only a few miles from the right bank of the Congo river. This should greatly encourage Bishop Taylor and his heroic band, and also the people who are giving their money and their loved ones to extend this blessed gospel in Africa.

This station is forty miles beyond Palaballa, and consists of seven buildings on three acres of land, which easily produce an abundant supply of plantains, maize and sweet potatoes, which in this, as in nearly all the stations, will furnish a large part of the food needed by the missionaries and their helpers and pupils. Mr. H. H. Johnston thinks that all the necessaries of life, in the line of food, may be raised in the stations; so that only luxuries need be imported from Europe and America. The natives are reached by preaching in the villages in the vicinity."

We may judge what can be done in mission work by the following report:

Among the most interesting of missionary premises anywhere, is the Moffat institute at Keomman in South Africa. The mission station rises like an oasis amid a desert of mirage-producing sands. There are its fruit trees, its pools of water, its growing corn, its village and its mission premises. The resident missionary is a son-in-law of the famous Robert Moffat. Moffat drained and cultivated this spot. His hands planted the healthy and varied fruit trees that flourished there. Quinces, grapes, apples, pears, peaches of unsurpassed quality abound. Thus Moffat turned his gardener's experience of early days to account. The mission buildings are of stone, and occupy the four sides of a square. The institute, in which ten youths are being educated for evangelistic work, is on the west side. North and south are the houses of the missionaries. On the east side is the home for the pupils. The chapel, ninety feet by twenty-five, is across the valley. There is a printing department at present issuing in the Batlaping dialect the Revised Verson of the New Testament. The work is done by natives who, as skilled artisans can take their place beside the printers in any community. The whole premises cost about sixty thousand dollars. Four medical missionaries are now laboring in Antananarivo, Madagascar, two of them in connection with the Norwegian Missionary Society, and two with the Friends' Foreign Association and the London Missionary Society conjointly. They have established a Medical Missionary Academy, successful candidates of which will be styled "Members of the Medical Missionary Academy." A hospital has been established, and a curriculum with annual examinations arranged for.—*Independent.*

NATIVE PREACHING.

In due time native preachers will be raised up, with "their native humor, quick religious sensibilities, musical voices, and loving hearts," which fit them for this work among their fellows. At a recent meeting in Westminister abbey, London, a member of the university's mission in Zanzibar stated that they had thirty-five native evangelists, formerly slaves, and among their converts is an earnest Christian youth, formerly page to the sultan of Zanzibar. The released slave had printed at their printing-office, the whole of the New Testament, and a large portion of the old in the Swahili language, understood throughout the interior. Before long missionaries will be sent to Africa from among the freedmen of this country. Already they have a list of classic names on the roll of African missions. Among these names stands that of Lott Carey, who was a slave in Virginia at the beginning of this century. He purchased freedom for himself and his children, gained an education and rose to great distinction as a preacher. He founded the 'Richmond African Baptist Missionary Society.' Going out as a missionary to Africa, he became foremost as a trusted statesman and leader of the people in the colony of Liberia. Another colored Baptist missionary, Rev. John Day, rendered eminent services in Liberia in many capacities from that of preacher to lieutenant-governor. It was George Licle, a colored native of Virginia, who was the first Baptist preacher of the West Indies. The first British missionary to Africa was a black man named Keith. Five or six colored missionaries were not long ago sent to Liberia under the care of the United States Foreign Mission Convention of the colored Baptists. In various Home Mission schools and universities, African missions receive prominent attention, and some among the bright, diligent sons and daughters of those who once were slaves, are preparing to tread African soil in the name of Jesus.

It has pleased God in each age and dispensation to set a representative of the Cushite race in some prominent light, even from before the days when at Moses' side sat Zipporah whom Miriam despised at her own peril. An Ethiopian rescued Jeremiah from the low dungeon. An Ethiopian under Candace, queen of his people, shines brightly in the firmament of Scripture history. It has been said that some results of his teaching of Gospel truth have in our day been traced out in the interior of Africa. Egypt and Libya had their share in the blessing and prophecy of Pentecost. I see in vision the princes of Egypt and the people of Ethiopia like the caravan of Sheba's queen, a 'very great train,' making haste to bring presents to the King of Salem. Perhaps among them is some honored legislator, some rapt musician who shall utter God's praises upon the harp, some dark-skinned Spurgeon, or some loving Lydia, who as a shining-eyed baby shall have been rescued with an offering of less than a score and a half of dollars from Mohammedan slavery in this present year,—this golden, result-freighted *now*.

'The King's business requires haste.' The time is at hand when Mohammedanism, strongly marshalled, and newly re-enforced, is advancing from the north and covetous and depraved adventurers, with firearms and strong drink, (for the International Congo Association, alas! does not decisively prohibit the liquor traffic), will press in on every side, upon the tribes where at present Christianity has a fair field against Fetichism. Yet for the fulfillment of God's plans concerning Africa, 'the stars in their courses' shall fight; and whether we stand on the side of those who 'willingly offer themselves among the people' in this great campaign, or stand aloof like Meroz, we may expect that, shaking off her long lethargy, Africa may soon take her place among nations now far in advance of her, and, supplementing their needs by her own especial resources and capabilities, may share richly in the blessing of a common Creator who, when He who shall declare, 'Blessed be Egypt my people, and Assyria the work of my hands, and Israel mine inheritance,' is able to perform his promise, for He is the Lord of Hosts."

Rum is ruin in Africa as everywhere else. A Mohammedan chief on the Niger was sent to petition Bishop Crowther, imploring him to prevent the sale of intoxicants among his people. He says: It is no long subject. It is about *barasa* (rum), *barasa, barasa, barasa*. My God! it has ruined our land; it has very, very much ruined our people, so that our people have become foolish. I have made a law that no one may buy or sell it, and that every one who is caught in selling it, his house shall be broken up; and that every one who is found drunk shall be killed: and have said to all Christian merchants that they may deal in everything except *barasa*. He goes on to beseech the bishop to help him, so that he can not only make these laws, but have them obeyed. For God's sake, and the prophet's sake, whom He has sent, the bishop must help us in this *barasa* matter! One has need of infinite faith in the power of the Gospel in the face of such an appeal from non-Christian people for protection against *Christian* (!) commerce. God help the right!

Northern Christian Advocate.

Lieutenant Kund, of the German African Society for the Congo, on foot, and with the help of the compass only, accompanied by a few Loango men, made a journey from Stanley Pool to the Kuango and Kassai, crossing the Sankulu, and going still farther north till he met a great river called the Ikatta which he followed northward and westward till it flowed through Lake Leopold (which he regards merely as *a lacustrine enlargement of the river*) out again into a stream called the Mfimi, which is simply a continuation of the Ikatta, and which he followed down to its confluence with the great Sankulu River, and thus with the Congo. *Service for the King.*

"DOMESTIC SLAVERY

Is so interwoven in the institutions of the country, that it would take generations to root it out; and I should more properly have called it domestic service. The natives are so well aware of the value of property, that slaves are often better treated than the members of the family. They carry on most of the commerce of their masters, often marry their daughters, and frequently become rich and powerful. Take, for example, the chief of Kintamo, Ngaliema. Originally a slave of Nchubila of Kinshassa, he is now the wealthiest ivory trader at Stanley Pool. It was this chief who threatened to stop Mr Stanley when he was advancing to create the station of Leopoldville. Now he is a warm ally; and not long ago, when two of his slaves ran away, taking with them some valuable ivory, he applied to the chief of Leopoldville for assistance. Sacrifices still take place on the death of a large chief, but not in the numbers one hears of on the Gold Coast.'

DOMESTIC LIFE.

Victor Hugo says: "Africa concerns the universe. Such a block-up of the traffic and circulation of mankind interferes with universal life. Human progress can no longer put up with the paralysis of a fifth part of the globe. The power of European thrones may develop the material resources of this pristine world, but the African home will determine the character of its people. Mothers and homes are the corner-stones of empires."

Hence the pertinent question of the hour is: What of woman and her social relations in Africa. Glance across the Atlantic to the kraal of a Kaffir wife, which is constructed on this wise. A circle eight or ten feet in diameter is drawn. Within this the women make the floor by pounding the clay until very hard, washing with manure and water, which renders it smooth and gives a polish. The men assist in setting poles in this circle, bending them over and tying with rope made of long grass. The height in the center is not more than four or five feet. After this frame work is completed, the women thatch it with coarse grass, leaving in one side an opening two feet high which serves for a door, chimney and window. For a fireplace, the housewife makes in the center of the floor a small circle with an elevated rim, to prevent the ashes and fire from scattering. She also fashions out the clay cooking utensils of various sizes, and bakes them. A finely woven rush mat, two feet square, serves for a table. Chairs are not needed, for all sit upon the floor. A beer strainer of braided rushes, a few wooden spoons, a wooden milk pail, hollowed out of a branch of a tree, two smooth stones for grinding corn, sleeping mats, blankets and wooden pillows prepared by the women, constitute the furniture.

Generally there are several wives in one household, and each has a separate kraal, or hut. These are built in a circle, enclosing a pen for cattle, and the doors open toward this fold. In these huts they cook the food for their dirty, unclad children, all eat with their fingers, at all hours, even to gluttony, drink beer, take snuff, and smoke. The wife tills the soil; she is the bread winner as well as the bread maker. In rainy weather she braids mats, grinds corn, pounds snuff and makes beer. In summer she takes her children with her to the bush for fuel and to the fields to cultivate corn and tobacco, while her husband lounges, smokes and gossips. One of the men was highly indignant when a missionary lady suggested that he might help his wife, who was pounding corn, with a baby strapped to her back. When a husband only regards his wife for her fruitfulness and usefulness there can be but little affection. She lavishes her affection on her children and will make great sacrifices to retain them with her."

"In Dahomey, the person of every female belongs to the king. Once every year he requires all marriageable girls to appear before him. He selects some for his harem, some for his guard, for some he chooses husbands, and the rest are returned to their parents.

His body guard is composed entirely of women, and is a regiment from twelve to twenty-five hundred strong. They are tall and more masculine in appearance than the male soldiers, and are better fighters, being possessed of unflinching courage and ruthless cruelty. When out on parade they are allowed to adorn themselves with the scalps of those they have slain in battle. On the death of a prince, many of his wives are slain, and if the number is not deemed sufficient, the king adds a selection of girls, who are painted white, and hung with ornaments. These sit about the coffin for days, but are finally doomed to the grave as attendants to the departed.

In Ashantee, the king is limited to three thousand three hundred and thirty-three wives, who during the working season, are scattered over his plantations, but in winter they occupy two streets in the capital, and are kept secluded.

Woman and slave are synonymous terms. They have no word for girl. Girls are "*woman boys.*" There is not, as in the Orient, lamentation at the birth of daughters. They are welcomed because an article of trade. A man sees a fortune in his daughters, a boy in his sisters. Why should he work? He is a lord, and it is his business to dispose of these girls to get wives for himself. The wife and children belong to the estate of the husband. When he dies they become the property of his family, to be disposed of as they choose, often separating mothers and children."

As Bishop Taylor is planting stations along the Congo and Kassai Rivers, the following from *The Baptist Missionary Magazine* will be read with interest:

"Col. Sir Francis DeWinton read a paper on June 7, before the Royal Geographical Society of Great Britian, in which he showed how steadily the work of exploration is being carried on and encouraged in the Congo Valley. He considers Lieut. Weissman's exploration the most important,

THE STEAMER "HENRY REED," UPPER CONGO.

FRIENDLY NATIVES. 89

which left the coast two years ago in two columns, and marched east for eight hundred miles and met in the Baluba country. They established a station, the king removing his capital to their neighborhood. Cattle were purchased, and seeds planted, and in six months they were in a prosperous condition. They had explored the Kassai River, and established themselves at the junction of the Kassai and Sulua, and built a fleet of canoes. The Kassai presents no difficulties to navigation. With its affluents, there is a large field for commerce and missions. Its average width is three-fourths of a mile, and the breadth of its valley from two to five miles, with hills of one hundred feet or so on either side. The india-rubber forest, bamboo palm, lined the banks for the first hundred miles; then the country became open prairie. The natives were similar to Congos, only a shade less civilized. They were, with one exception, friendly and engaged in trade. He thinks, after two years spent in the country, that the Free State has no reason for apprehension from the black races. He thinks them negative races, possessing neither gratitude, affection, nor courage, not even having vicious kind of vices. They are not naturally cruel, nor as a rule treacherous, and bear no malice if punished justly. They will lie and steal from the white man, and are cunning and suspicious. He says:

'During the two years I was on the Congo, I never experienced any trouble. To govern them, they must respect you. My predecessor, Mr. Stanley, was respected; and I succeeded to the heritage. If a native does not fear you, he jumps to the opposite conclusion,— that you fear him; and then trouble arises. I continued Mr. Stanley's policy; and, while I endeavored to be respected,

I on my part respected their manners and customs. If punishment was necessary, I punished as far as possible in conformity with their own laws. In thus ruling them, you obtain their confidence and respect; and that once gained, there is as little difficulty in governing a million of such people as in governing a thousand. Their chief characteristic is their love for commerce; they are born traders. The women do all the hard work and the agricultural labor; while the men look after the children, and do what sewing is required. Thus the labor of the two sexes is almost reversed; yet, in spite of this, the women retain some of the well-known attributes of their sex.

The second reason — their tribal formation — demands only a short explanation. You will easily understand that in a country made up of small communities, where a few villiages constitute a kingdom, where autonomy is the law of the land, where every one is weak and no one is strong, where there is no unity, no strong hand by which nations are made and kingdoms created, — a settled form of government on European principles will meet with no great difficulties from a native population. I think this fact, and the natives love of trade, are the two most important factors in the future of the new state. The one guarantees security, and the other invites commerce."

No doubt millions of poor Africans are reaching out their hands to God for the light of the glorious Gospel. Read the following:

"The captain of a river steamer on the Lower Niger states that in every trip during the last two years the natives, among whom a missionary is unknown, have boarded his ship with the invariable question: 'Is God palavar man aboard?' or,

'When is He coming?' 'If he come to teach us so that we know white man's book, then we build him a house and school and give him chop — plenty.' The Roman Catholics are said to be ready to occupy this field."

Modern Inventions for Africa.

We are glad to learn that some of the most remarkable of recent inventions are being introduced into the depths of Africa. A telephone line along the Congo is being placed for a long distance. Bishop Taylor's steamer is being carried up the Congo, "and with it the electric light will make its advent on the river, turning night into day wherever it goes." H. M. Stanley carries a Maxim repeating gun, to keep the natives at a respectful distance. De Brazza is introducing portable bridges, by which he hopes to successfully pass through the treacherous fords or the clumsy ferries. A company has been organized to build a railroad around the Congo Falls.

At the same time Bishop Taylor is establishing twelve missions in Liberia, where the native chiefs agree to build mission houses and school-houses, and plant various kinds of fruits before the missionaries arrive, and fifty missionaries are called for, including a man and wife for each of these stations, and these are to leave New York next October.

The chiefs also agree to give the missionaries land for farming and grazing purposes. Bishop Taylor agrees to furnish teachers and preachers, and all else that is required to put the work on a self-supporting basis. Six of these stations are up the Cavilla river, which flows into the Atlantic eighteen miles S. E. of Cape Palmas. Bishop Taylor says: "Some of these stations are at the river business towns of large inland tribes. These missions are all in a most fertile country, five of them on the high banks of a river which is open to steamboat navigation, and as free from sluggish creeks and swamps, and as healthy as the Hudson river, N. Y."

White men and women are wanted for teachers, of good constitution and common sense, and if they take nine hours for sleep every night, and sabbath rest every week, Bishop Taylor says, "It would be safe to insure their lives for ten years in a land where there are no drug stores or M. D.s." He says, "This is the most beautiful tropical climate I ever visited." Another writer says, "Liberia is not only the most fertile, salubrious, and beautiful section of West Africa, but it has convenient access to the wealthiest districts of the Niger valley. It is not difficult for a man of the least energy to make a comfortable living." Bishop Gilbert Haven said, "Let Liberia fill up her land with farmers, and she will conquer Africa."

Mrs. Amanda Smith writes from Africa:

"For two weeks now, I have been on a tour with Bishop Taylor, together with a party of seven others. We left Cape Palmas last Monday, and the Bishop has established five stations on this river. This is a beautiful river, wide and long. You may gather some little idea of its scenery if you have gone up and down the Hudson river; but its beauty is indescribable. We have grand talks from the Bishop. We gather around him like a lot of birds with mouths and ears open to catch every word at any moment he has. He is never idle a moment, scarcely. At Baruka, where we were two weeks ago, the Bishop went with the men to clear off the land; he used the axe as easily as if he had done nothing else all his life. I praise God for such a godly example of industry for our young men and everybody else. Last night, Sunday, the Bishop had the people called together in this town, and he gave them a talk, then the rest of us gave a little experience and talk. Oh, they were so interested! and we sang and prayed and had a blessed time in prayer. I felt the Lord had answered. This town is among the heathen. If the Bishop had men to take the place, he could easily settle a number of beautiful places with different tribes. The doors are open everywhere. Amen!"

THE LIGHTING OF THE "DARK CONTINENT."

"To the regions beyond, pass the truth-telling wires
  O'er the sea where old Tyre sat, a purple-robed queen;
Stretch lines o'er the desert, and kindle keen fires,
  Where the Niger rolls broadly 'mid valleys of green.

Lift up the deep voice of your cataract waves,
  Ye floods of the Congo! her woods, clap your hands!
The feet of swift messengers gleam by the graves
  Where sleep the first heralds from occident lands.

Wake, shores of Zambesi! wake, bright inland seas!
  They come,—Heaven's ambassadors bringing good-will;
Peace, daughters of bondage! they speak your release!
  Rise, clan of Sechele! for the war-cry is still.

He came—your Redeemer—to drink sorrow's cup;
  He rose, sending love thoughts to every domain;
He comes yet in glory—sad faces (!) look up
  To wait His appearing, and welcome his reign."

CHAPTER VI.

FACTS ABOUT LIBERIA.

Liberia is the name given to that region of country on the west coast of Africa, lying between 4° 20' and 7° 30' north latitude. It contains 97,000 square miles. It was founded by the American Civilization Society in 1820. It became an independent state in 1847. The constitution is modelled after that of the United States. All men are born free and equal. The natives are robust, healthy and long-lived. The dry season lasts from October to June, and the wet season from June to October. The average heat of the dry season is 84, seldom rising to 90 degrees in the shade. The average heat of the wet season is 76, never falling below 60 degrees.

The colonists write as follows: "A more fertile soil, and more productive country, so far as it is cultivated, there is not, we believe, on the face of the earth. Its hills and plains are covered with verdure that never fails. The productions of nature keep on in their growth through all the seasons of the year. The natives, without farming tools, without skill, and with little labor, raise more grain and vegetables than they can consume, and often more than they can sell. There is no dreary winter, for one-half of the year, in which they consume the products of the other. Nature is constantly renewing herself, and constantly pouring her treasures *all the year round* in the laps of the industrious."

Governor Ashmun says: "One acre of rich land will produce $300 worth of indigo, half an acre can be made to grow half a ton of arrowroot. Two crops of corn, sweet potatoes and other vegetables may be raised yearly."

The forests contain teak, mahogany, rosewood, hickory, poplar, several kinds of gum trees, dye-woods, medicinal shrubs, and a variety of useful palms, including the nut bearing palm, from which palm oil is made.

The wild animals, including the elephant, hippopotamus, crocodile and leopard, are almost exterminated.

Iron abounds, copper is found in the interior, and gold is found in considerable quantities.

Fruits abound, including plantains, bananas, oranges, sousop, twenty varieties of prunes, guava, pawpaw, pineapple, grape, and the tropical peach and cherry.

Vegetables abound, including sweet potatoes, cassada, yams, cocoa, ground nuts, arrowroot, egg plant, ochre, and every variety of beans, with peas, cucumbers, and pumpkins.

Grains are found, including Indian corn, coffee, pepper of three varieties equal to cayenne, millet, quinca, corn. The sugar corn grows luxuriantly. Cotton yields two crops annually.

The weather is delightful. In December it is not very warm during the day, and cool enough at night to sleep under a blanket. With proper precautions, and under moderate prudence the people from any northern state can live in this country with little fear from the weather.

Mr. Ashmun, one of the first governors, says: "No situation in West Africa can be more salubrious than that of Montserado. The night air does all that can be done for it in this climate. The night air is nearly as pure as any other."

Monrovia is the capital, and contains 13,000 inhabitants. Its location is the most delightful that can be imagined. It is a flourishing city, having a fort, a light-house, a commercial market, schools, churches, newspapers, charitable associations, and other institutions like those of the United States. Industrial processes, and manufactories have started among them.

Liberia is divided into four counties, Mesurado, Grand Bassa, Sinou and Maryland. The annual exports have amounted to $1,000,000. They are chiefly palm oil, ivory, tortoise shell, hides, gold, and a variety of dyewoods. The total population is 720,000, of whom 19,000 are American Liberians, and the rest natives. The American Liberians have a regular system of schools, and are progressing in various branches of civilization.

Henry M. Stanley has often visited Liberia, and speaks of this young Republic as follows:

"The American people had evidently forgotten that it was through the philanthropy of their fellow citizens that the free State of Liberia had been founded, to the establishment of which they had contributed $2,558,987 of their money to create homes and comforts for the 18,000 free Africans they dispatched to settle there. This State *they might regard with honest pride.* It was an act well worthy of the great Republic, not only as taking the lead in publicly recognizing and supporting the great work of African civilization in history, and in promoting the extension of commerce, but of significant import *in view of its interest for the future weal of the seven millions of people of African descent within its borders.*"

The St. Paul's river empties itself into the Liberian Bay. About 20 miles from its mouth there is a water-fall, above which the river is navigable for 200 or 300 miles. The Mesurado River is 40 miles long, and enters the sea on the north side of the cape of the same name. Forty miles S. E. of Cape Mesurado are two considerable rivers, one descending from N. N. W., and the other from E. N. E., and pouring their waters into the ocean, at a distance of only two miles from each other.

The St. John's River is larger than any that we have mentioned. It is navigable for vessels of 90 to 100 tons, abounding with fish, and having its course through a fertile, delicious and salubrious country, of rich and mellow soil, fanned by a sea breeze 16 hours in every 24. Even in the dry season, this breeze is tempered and sweetened in its passage up the river by the verdure which crowns its banks, rendering the scene one of the most delightful that can be imagined.

BISHOP WILLIAM TAYLOR IN LIBERIA.

The Christian world is more interested in Liberia just now because Bishop Taylor has just located seventeen mission stations in that lovely land, and calls for fifty missionaries to go there next October. He has entered into a covenant with the kings and head men of these tribes or nations, and they bind themselves to give him the choice of all the land he needs for building, farming, and for grazing purposes, and to plant the first crop for plenty of food for the missionaries; to provide materials and build a good cook-house and school-house, to cut and carry hard wood pillars and all the framing timber for a good American house at each station for the residence of missionaries, and to do all these things cheerfully and free of charge. These agreements have been entered into after due deliberation; and in return the Bishop engages to furnish men and women for these stations, and to furnish the material for covering the frames of these American houses, and see that these missionaries are at these stations by January 1st, 1888.

The Bishop found that they nearly all wanted white men and women to teach them, for they have not so much faith in men of their own color. The Bishop writes: "Five of these stations are on the Cavalla River, which is nearly as large as the Hudson River, N. Y., and flows rapidly between high banks, no swamps, and is beautifully clean."

Mrs. Amanda Smith went with Bishop Taylor in planting these missions, and she was so delighted with the lovely hills along this Cavalla River on which she would build a house and settle down, that she screamed with rapture of admiration, and often shouted, "Glory to God!" This river flows into the Atlantic 18 miles east of Cape Palmas.

The first station up this river is Eubloko, a small town, but the river depot of a large tribe, with many towns in the interior. The articles were signed by King Nebly and King Pacey, also by several chiefs. The mission building will occupy a high bluff overlooking the river, and high hills in the background having good soil. All this region is fertile, high, hilly and healthful. The Bishop writes: "The natives are as naked and destitute of clothing as the tribes I met on the Congo, with this advantage: many of the young men of these tribes are sailors, and can speak broken English, 'patwa,' so that I found some who could interpret in every place."

The next station as we ascend this river is Yawki Darabo. The site of the mission house is a large mound shaped hill a quarter of a mile from the river, but in full view. It will have a good landing of its own. The articles were signed by King Wohpasara, and a number of the chiefs.

The third station up this river is Beaboo, very much like the other two stations below. The Bishop had a good time preaching to the kings Yasahnoo and Tahlee, and the chiefs, after the business council closed.

The next station is Taba Tateka, on the east bank of the river, a town of some hundreds of people. The big town of the Tabo tribe is nearly a day's march inland, easterly. Our mission building will occupy a hill half a mile north, having a far-reaching view of the river.

Brother J. S. Pratt, the mission agent for Bishop Taylor, has a trading post here at Tateka, and also at Gerobo. Mr. Pratt had told the people that Bishop Taylor was coming, and they waited with great eagerness, and when the Bishop arrived, King Krahoriri jumped and shouted like an old sinner just converted to God, and a good part of the evening was spent in the discharge of muskets and the beating of drums.

The next station is Gerobo, and is 70 miles from the sea, where King Grandoo, and chiefs Cesar, Biscya, Burraba, Kapa and Payoo signed the articles. The Bishop writes: "Then under escort we marched 12 miles inland to the big town of Wahlaky, passing through two towns of the same tribes on our way.

"We spent two nights at Wahlaky. They supplied us plentifully with flesh and fowl. We saw the people sacrificing to devils in their large council-house, saw their devil-dances, marching, shouting, and firing of guns, which was kept up nearly all day. Then we had a large company of them to hear us sing praises to God. Amanda Smith gave them a long talk about Jesus and salvation. The king and his chiefs signed our articles. We returned the next day to Gerobo, and the next day we descended the river, stopping to visit all the stations we had opened.

"Baraka is a large village 12 miles from Cape Palmas. When we visited this place to establish a station, I slept in the open air, as I did at all the places, but Sisters Smith, Tubman and Fletcher occupied one of the best houses in the town. It was nearly 30 feet in diameter, round as a perfect circle, with an upper story reached by a movable ladder to a bamboo platform seven feet up, where a permanent ladder led to the upper apartment, which was used for stores of rice and other supplies; all around were pins and hooks and sacks, and all laden with stores, showing the industry and ingenuity, economy and thrift of the owner, but no owner appeared. This was the house of the king's first wife, who had been accused of witchcraft, and had fled to escape being put to death. She returned, and was compelled to drink poison, but appealed to God to spare her life if she was innocent. Her prayer was answered, and those of the missionaries, and when it was proved that she was innocent there was great rejoicing for a number of days."

Hear the Bishop's pleading and mark his plans:

"Why cannot my people, my dear people of America, my Methodist people in large numbers give themselves to God for the redemption of Africa? Why should these blood-bought souls continue to sit in darkness when we can reach them so easily, yet revel at home? In each of the seven places we have named, we will (D. V.) between this and Christmas of this year, build a small but healthy mission house for a young man and his wife. Each house will be 22x24 feet, divided into two rooms, and a veranda in front 10x14 feet, which will answer for receiving-room, dining-room and general family purposes. A few years hence, it will be easy to add 36 feet to it, giving a hall 12x12 through the centre, with two 12x12 rooms at each end, and veranda in front 10x60 feet, and a similar one in the rear enclosed for a girls' dormitory, 10x60 feet, to accommodate 30 to 40 girls under the immediate care of the matron. Our boys will live in neatly arranged native houses built with their own hands."

Thus he has provided for 17 stations which we have no space to name, but to show the eagerness of the people for the gospel mark the following from the king of Pickenny Sess, where the Bishop did not call when he passed up to Settra Kroo:

"RT. REV. WM. TAYLOR: We regret very much that you passed us on your way to Settra Kroo.

After hearing you at Grand Sess our hearts were very glad; but after you passed us our hearts were very sad. We must say, dear Bishop, come back here. We are about 6000 in number, and about 8000 children who have never heard the gospel sound. Come back, Bishop, we will build you a house, and give you as much land as you want, and pay your teachers just to teach our children. We had already picked a place for you, so that we beg you come back."

        Signed King Sanier and his head men.

The Bishop accepts this station, and J. S. Pratt will submit to them the articles to sign.

On the Kroo coast the tribes are larger, and more missionaries will be needed, so the mission houses will be larger, being uniformly 36x28 feet, giving a centre hall 12x22 feet, and two rooms at each end 11x12 feet, and a 6 foot veranda the whole length of the building in front.

Fifteen young men and their wives, if they have any, are required to man these stations. Holy men are wanted, "apt to teach," either missionaries or young men who have the woe upon them, if they preach not the gospel, they must also be willing to take the first row in the Industrial School Department as well. Four of them will land at Grand Bassa, and the rest at Cape Palmas. Bro. J. S. Pratt and Sister Amanda Smith will receive them, and help them to their stations.

When Bishop Taylor was appointed Bishop of Africa, he laid down his life on the altar of Africa, and expected to die. But he has entirely changed his mind in regard to the perils of life in Africa, especially in Liberia, which he believes is a healthy climate, much more so than the eastern shore of

VILLAGE ON THE WEST COAST OF AFRICA. A PALAVER TREE.

**BOSTON UNIVERSITY
COLLEGE OF LIBERAL ARTS
LIBRARY**

Maryland, New Jersey, or New York, and far ahead of the new settlements in the valley of the Mississippi. "It is an equable, salubrious and enjoyable climate, with no plague of flies, and but few mosquitoes."

To give the missionaries every advantage possible, the mission houses will be carefully built with sills five feet above the ground. Bishop Taylor says, "If the missionaries are of good constitution, and will conform to the laws of health, especially securing nightly and Sabbath rest, and regular work in our school industries, we shall have but a small death-roll to call."

After penning the above lines I opened my Bible to Acts 28 : 28, and read, "Be it known therefore unto you, that the salvation of God is sent unto the Gentiles, and that they will hear it." And again, "All the ends of the earth shall remember and return unto the Lord." And again, "I will open rivers in high places, and fountains in the midst of the valleys: I will make the wilderness a pool of water, and the dry land springs of water, that they may see and know, and consider and understand together, that the hand of the Lord hath done this, and the Holy One of Israel hath created it." Isaiah 41 : 18-20.

Our missionaries on the Cavalla River can visit each other by canoe at short notice, which will be a great comfort.

Some of these tribes received and entertained the Bishop and his party after the style of the days of Abraham. But two of the tribes seemed to think that missions meant money for them. They tried to bleed for gain.

The Bishop wisely observes: "The civilization of the coast is strong enough to release the natives within its lines from the restraints of heathen law, which guarantees protection against thieves, but not strong enough to substitute adequate moral force to give protection to anything that thieves can covet or carry away. Our alternatives are, under God, to make a success on the self-supporting line, using the money given us to establish early and adequate self-support, on a scale commensurate with the demands of the work, or an indefinite postponement of Africa's evangelization through the centuries that may ensue."

Mrs. J. R. Roberts, the widow of the first president of Liberia, is collecting money for a general hospital, to be located at Monrovia, the capital of the Republic. Mrs. Roberts was very kindly received by President Cleveland, who became the first contributor toward the proposed hospital.

Dr. Oscar Lentz, the eminent scientist, has returned to Europe, after travelling on foot across the African Continent, through regions literally reeking with marsh fevers, agues and small-pox. During the entire journey he enjoyed robust health, and not once felt the need of medicine. Not a drop of alcoholic liquor passed his lips. Rice, chicken and tea formed his staple fare, and he dressed entirely in flannel.

Dr. J. W. Lugonbeal, late colonial physician and United States agent in Liberia, gives the following important information:

"On the whole, I regard the climate of Liberia as decidedly pleasant, notwithstanding the scorching rays of the tropical sun, and the abundance of rain which falls during the year. So far as the pleasantness of the climate is concerned, I would decidedly prefer a residence in Liberia to one in any part of the United States."

HABITS CONDUCIVE TO HEALTH.

The above doctor speaks of the importance of those who go to Liberia of being careful as to their *habits, diet and clothing* to the extent of exposure to the heat of the day as well as to the damp and chilling night air, and especially to the avoidance of all sources of mental inquietude, and of the care that should be taken to send out as missionaries only such persons as are of sound body and of a quiet mind.

He well says, " Whoever goes to Africa ough to go with the *expectation of living*, and should be cheerful and contented if they should be sick, and avoid all gloomy forebodings."

He says, " I seldom failed to break up the fever in a few days by the judicious use of quinine. I usually administered two grains at a time." He is decidedly of the opinion that cold water is the best beverage. Mark the following:

He adds: " I am quite satisfied that everything which is really necessary for human subsistence and comfort, together with many luxuries, can be secured in Liberia with much less labor than would be required to procure the necessaries of life in the United States. Let the cultivation of the soil receive that attention which it should receive as the principal means of wealth, and the citizens of Liberia may live in ease and comfort and independence."

WORKS OF REV. E. DAVIES.

THE GIFT OF THE HOLY GHOST, AND SELECT SERMONS. Price, enamel paper covers, 50 cents; cloth, 80 cts.
"*It is just the book for the masses*, and cannot fail to do good." —*Bishop R. S. Foster.*

THE BELIEVER'S HANDBOOK ON HOLINESS. Containing eight Lectures. 12mo. Price, enamel paper, 25 cts.; cloth, 40 cents.
"*This is truly an excellent work.* Most heartily do we commend it to all."—*Mrs. Phebe Palmer.*

THE GIFT OF THE HOLY GHOST AND BELIEVER'S HANDBOOK. In One volume. Cloth, $1.

THE BOY PREACHER, OR THE LIFE AND LABORS OF REV. THOMAS HARRISON. Fine Steel Portrait. Price, $1, Enlarged Edition.
"A wonderful record of God's marvellous works."

GEMS AND PEARLS, FOR PARENTS AND CHILDREN. For Family Reading and Sabbath schools. Fine Steel Engraving. Price 75 cents.
"Rev. E Davies has collected a goodly number of Gems and Pearls. *Many of them are severally worth the price of the book.* Read it."—*Dr. Fowler, in New York Christian Advocate.*

THE LAW OF HOLINESS. AN EXPOSITION OF THE TEN COMMANDMENTS. Showing the relation of the Decalogue to the Gospel and to the Moral Universe. Large 16mo. Price 75 cents.
"It is *clear, sharp*, and discriminating. It gives a practical application of the moral law to the duties of Christian life, and is a fresh presentation of this important subject." — *Rev. J. A. Wood*

DAILY FOOD FOR CHRISTIAN WORKERS. Price 15 cents; gilt edges, 20 cents; paper, 10 cents.
It is adapted to the highest experiences of Christian life.

CONTRAST BETWEEN CHRISTIANITY AND INFIDELITY. A Book of Reference for Ministers and Christian Workers. Price, paper, 20 cents; cloth, 40 cents.
"This book is *worthy of a place in any Library.*" — *Lutheran Observer.*

SELECTIONS FROM HARRIS' MAMMON. An invaluable book. Price 10 cents.

MEMOIRS AND JOURNAL OF MRS. HESTER ANN ROGERS. Condensed and combined. Price, cloth, 50 cents.

LIFE OF FRANCES RIDLEY HAVERGAL. With choice selections from her writings. Price only 50 cents; gilt, 75 cts.
"No Christian can read this biography without acquiring a sharp appetite for the heavenly manna on which this saint of God fed, and grew so strong and beautiful." — *Rev. D. Steele, D.D.*

Any book sent by mail on receipt of price.

HOLINESS BOOK CONCERN, Reading, Mass.

AN ILLUSTRATED HAND BOOK ON AFRICA.

GIVING AN ACCOUNT OF ITS PEOPLE, ITS CLIMATE, ITS RESOURCES, ITS DISCOVERIES, RIVERS, LAKES. AND SOME OF ITS MISSIONS. PRICE, TWENTY-FIVE CENTS.

Testimonials.

Rev. Daniel Steele, D. D., writes: "I have read your ILLUSTRATED HAND BOOK ON AFRICA with great interest. Not many people have time to read Stanley's large volumes, and a still smaller number can afford to own them. Your Hand Book, scattered widely among Christian people, will awaken our interest in the great enterprise of the evangelization of the dark continent. I hope you will be called upon for a hundred thousand copies."

"Our enterprising and indefatigable co-laborer, Rev. E. Davies, has published an ILLUSTRATED HAND BOOK ON AFRICA. We have read it several times, studied the newly made map, looked at the striking pictures, and it is surprising to see the amount of valuable information he has gathered so rapidly together." And again, "Not one person interested in Bishop Taylor's work ought to be without this Hand Book. It contains ninety large pages of excellent reading, ten illustrations, and a map of the New Congo State." Rev. E. I. D. Pepper, in *Christian Standard*.

"Those who have not access to larger works will find this very useful, as giving a good deal of information in a brief space touching Africa, its rivers, lakes, animals, inhabitants, idolatries, and products." *Christian Standard*, Cincinnati.

"Rev. E. Davies, as a compiler of books, exhibits a degree of energy and activity quite on a par with his chosen profession of an evangelist at large. In the harvest field, where he has met with a large and substantial measure of success. For Bishop Taylor and his missions, Bro. Davies has evinced uncommon interest; this led him to prepare and publish a popular life sketch of the great missionary. Now he has written and published an ILLUSTRATED HAND BOOK ON AFRICA. The appearance of such a publication just at this juncture is timely, not only for the specific information it contains for those who may join their fortunes with Bishop Taylor, but for the general public, who are without access to the sources of such historical and geographical facts as are grouped in this convenient form." Dr. A. Wallace in *Ocean Grove Record*.

HOLINESS BOOK CONCERN, READING, MASS.

LIFE OF WM. TAYLOR,
BISHOP OF AFRICA.
BY REV. E. DAVIES.

Illustrated with a Fine Steel Portrait, Three Pictures of Africa and One of Ceylon.

PRICE, SEVENTY-FIVE CENTS.

OPINIONS OF THE PRESS.

"This is a spirited book by an earnest admirer of the latest, and, in an eminent sense, the best of all the African explorers. As a trumpet call to the Church, we expect good to come of this volume."—*Daniel Curry, D. D., LL.D.*

"It is an interesting and soul-inspiring volume."—*Dr. Cullis.*

"We have seldom found a book which has stirred our souls as this one has done. There is that in it which will inspire faith, courage, confidence. There is a vast amount of information concerning Africa. This is one of the books that will live. The author, with his usual tact, has succeeded in bringing together the chief items of interest in the mission work of this modern apostle; and the man and his work stand out before the reader upon its pages."—*Chicago Free Methodist.*

"The book is entertainingly written and sufficiently full to give the reader an intelligent acquaintance with its subject."

"The book presents the truth in *distinct out-line*, and will do good, and only good to the careful reader."

"This book needs no commendation to sell it. It sketches rapidly the early life and labors, and, more largely, the recent history of Bishop Taylor."

"It contains 216 pages and a fine steel portrait of the remarkable man who is pursuing his way into the interior of Africa."

"The remarkable life story of the heroic evangelist who is now directing the Methodist forces into the heart of Africa, is told by Rev. E. Davies. Many will be glad to know that the life of Bishop Taylor can be obtained in so compendious a form as it is here presented."—*S. S. Times.*

HOLINESS BOOK CONCERN, READING, MASS.

TESTIMONIALS

ON

The Life of Rev. John Wesley by Rev. E. Davies, 261 pages, 12 mo., five illustrations. Fifty cents, paper; seventy-five cents, cloth.

"Mr. Davies has disposed of his material to good advantage, and produced a most readable book. He furnishes a good outline of the early life, collegiate career, spiritual experience, evangelistic labors of John Wesley, and of the organization which perpetuates his name and work."—*The Wesleyan, Halifax.*

"There is unquestionably a place for this book, and we doubt not it will be well received."—*North Western Christian Advocate.*

"It is compiled from the latest biographies, and makes a very entertaining and profitable volume, giving a good outline of his early life, his college days, religious experience, evangelistic labors, the founding of his societies, his doctrines, extended ministry, and the closing incidents of his eventful life. It will be read with interest and profit."—*Zion's Herald.*

"The author has succeeded in giving us a well-written and interesting volume."—*The Free Methodist.*

"We have just finished reading Rev. E. Davies' 'Life of Wesley.' It is glorious, reading of God's wonderful dealings with his servant. The power of God came down as I finished reading the book, and I shouted and praised the Lord." —Capt. R. KELSO CARTER.

"The greatness of the character of John Wesley, and the depth of his consecration, have overflowed all denominational lines. This volume deals with the leading facts of his life. It is good for the closet and the study."—*The Contributor.*

This book is illustrated, and gives a large amount of very interesting matter concerning the life of this man of God, which should be read by all church members, of whatever denomination.

HOLINESS BOOK CONCERN,
READING, MASS.

www.ingramcontent.com/pod-product-compliance
Lightning Source LLC
Chambersburg PA
CBHW020106170426
43199CB00009B/410